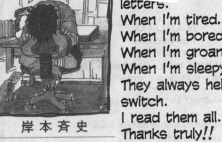

...u for your constant fan letters.
When I'm tired...
When I'm bored...
When I'm groaning in pain...
When I'm sleepy...
They always help to flip my heart's switch.
I read them all.
Thanks truly!!

岸本斉史

—Masashi Kishimoto, 2000

Author/artist Masashi Kishimoto was born in 1974 in rural Okayama Prefecture, Japan. After spending time in art college, he won the Hop Step Award for new manga artists with his manga **Karakuri** ("Mechanism"). Kishimoto decided to base his next story on traditional Japanese culture. His first version of **Naruto**, drawn in 1997, was a one-shot story about fox spirits; his final version, which debuted in **Weekly Shonen Jump** in 1999, quickly became the most popular ninja manga in Japan.

NARUTO

3-in-1 Edition
Volume 2
SHONEN JUMP Manga Omnibus Edition
A compilation of the graphic novel volumes 4–6

STORY AND ART BY MASASHI KISHIMOTO

Translation/Katy Bridges, Mari Morimoto
English Adaptation/Jo Duffy
Touch-up Art & Lettering/Heidi Szykowny
Design/Sean Lee (Manga Edition)
Design/Sam Elzway (Omnibus Edition)
Editors/Jason Thompson, Shaenon K. Garrity, Frances E. Wall (Manga Edition)
Senior Editor/Megan Bates (Manga Edition)
Senior Editor/Joel Enos (Omnibus Edition)

Printed in the U.S.A.

Published by VIZ Media, LLC
P.O. Box 77010
San Francisco, CA 94107

10 9 8
Omnibus edition first printing, July 2011
Eighth printing, September 2017

www.viz.com

RATED T FOR TEEN
PARENTAL ADVISORY
NARUTO is rated T for Teen and is recommended for ages 13 and up. This volume contains realistic and fantasy violence.
ratings.viz.com

www.shonenjump.com

SHONEN JUMP MANGA EDITION

NARUTO

VOL. 4

HERO'S BRIDGE

STORY AND ART BY

MASASHI KISHIMOTO

SAKURA サクラ

Smart and studious, Sakura is the brightest of Naruto's classmates, but she's constantly distracted by her crush on Sasuke. Her goal: to win Sasuke's heart!

NARUTO ナルト

When Naruto was born, a destructive fox spirit was imprisoned inside his body. Spurned by the older villagers, he's grown into an attention-seeking troublemaker. His goal: to become the village's next *Hokage*.

SASUKE サスケ

The top student in Naruto's class, Sasuke comes from the prestigious Uchiha clan. His goal: to get revenge on a mysterious person who wronged him in the past.

KAKASHI カカシ

The elite ninja assigned to train Naruto, Sasuke, and Sakura. His *sharingan* ("mirror-wheel eye") allows him to reflect and mimic enemy *ninjutsu*.

ZABUZA 再不斬

A ruthless ninja assassin and mass-murderer known as "The Demon." He specializes in techniques involving water and mist.

HAKU 白

A mysterious orphan who befriends Naruto. Naruto doesn't realize that his new friend is Zabuza's loyal masked assistant, who fights with chiropractic needles.

TAZUNA タズナ

An old bridge-builder struggling to bring prosperity to the Land of Waves. The evil millionaire Gato has hired Zabuza to stop him from completing his newest bridge.

THE STORY SO FAR...

Twelve years ago, a destructive nine-tailed fox spirit attacked the ninja village of Konohagakure. The *Hokage*, or village champion, defeated the fox by sealing its soul into the body of a baby boy. Now that boy, Uzumaki Naruto, has grown up to become a ninja-in-training, learning the art of *ninjutsu* with his classmates Sakura and Sasuke.

Tired of easy exercises, Naruto and his classmates make the mistake of asking their teacher, Kakashi, for a really hard assignment... and find themselves in the Land of Waves, protecting a bridge-builder named Tazuna. But the job turns truly dangerous when the notorious assassin Zabuza shows up. While Kakashi holds off Zabuza and Sakura protects Tazuna, Naruto and Sasuke face Zabuza's assistant Haku. In the battle, Sasuke sacrifices himself to save Naruto from Haku's deadly throwing needles. Now, watching his classmate fall, Naruto feels something terrible stir within him...

CONTENTS

28: NINE TAILS...!!

WH...WHAT CHAKRA IS THIS?!

!

ONG ONG ONG

SHFF

!!

Number 28: Nine Tails...!!

READ THIS WAY

...IMPOSSIBLE...!! HIS CHAKRA IS PHYSICALLY MANIFESTING ITSELF!
...A-AND AN APPALLING CHAKRA IT IS!

FSSSST

SS

SS

!
...HIS HAND... THE WOUNDS ARE... HEALING THEMSELVES!

WHO- WHAT ON EARTH IS HE?!!
ONNNNG

!!

!!

!

...!!
IS THIS... ZABUZA'S DOING?!

!!
NO!
NO... THIS POWER – THIS ENERGY... IS... FOUL... IT'S EVIL AND... FAMILIAR... BUT IT CAN'T BE!

READ THIS WAY

NARUTO!!
UNBELIEVABLE. IT CAN'T BE! AFTER ALL THIS TIME--

KAKASHI...?!
NO... IT SEEMS BIGGER THAN KAKASHI, SOMEHOW. BUT WHO--?!

THIS CHAKRA I'M FEELING. SOMETHING ABOUT IT... FILLS ME WITH DREAD!

-HAS THE BINDING SPELL BEGUN TO UNRAVEL? IS THE SEAL BROKEN?

!
...

I SENSE THAT WE'RE SAFE - FOR NOW. IT HASN'T BROKEN THROUGH YET... NOT COMPLETELY.
BUT THE SEAL HAS SLIPPED A LITTLE, OR CRACKED. AND THE POWER OF THE NINE-TAILED DEMON FOX IS BLEEDING THROUGH.

...I SENSE...

ZOOOM

IF I ACT QUICKLY, THERE'S STILL A CHANCE --!

LISTEN TO ME... ZABUZA...
...I'M A BUSY MAN. YOU'RE A BUSY MAN. WE'VE BOTH GOT A LOT ON OUR PLATES...

READ THIS WAY
... AND IT GOES AGAINST THE GRAIN TO EVEN SUGGEST THIS...
...BUT WHAT DO YOU SAY WE STOP SCREWING AROUND...
FWUP FWP FWP FWP
POK
...AND WRAP THIS UP RIGHT NOW? ONE BIG MOVE, WINNER TAKE ALL?
BAM
AN INTRIGUING NOTION...
WHAT'S LEFT, KAKASHI?
SHOW ME WHAT YOU'VE GOT!
GONGONGONG

GRRRR

HE'S ATTACKING!!!
CHUK
TAK

FWOOSH!
HE'S SO BLOODTHIRSTY! HE'S COMPLETELY CHANGED FROM THE BOY OF JUST MINUTES AGO!
RAAAAR
POW!
HE... HE DEFLECTED THEM... WITHOUT EVEN TOUCHING THEM?!
FWOOM
!
GLARE

BOOOOOM
TUMBLE
THUD
I'VE GOT TO MAKE IT TO THE NEXT MIRROR!
TAK

FWHHH
SHLUK!!
GRRRRRR
HE COULDN'T HAVE--!!

AAAUUURGH!!

ONGONGONG

THIS IS BAD!!!
PLIT
PLIT
I CAN'T WITHSTAND HIS CHAKRA ANY MORE!!!
!
PLIT
OW...
KRUNCH
UHN...
HEH
!!

SKID SKID SKID
KRAK
SHHM

READ THIS WAY

SNAP
SNAP
POP

POP
PING
SNAP

PING
PING

SHHF

...MASTER ZABUZA...
PING

!!

TAK
...I...
...AM FINISHED.

MASTER ZABUZA...
PING

KISHIMOTO MASASHI'S FIRST MANGA REJECT SPECIAL!

THE CHARACTER DESIGNS TO THE LEFT ARE FROM A FAILED PROJECT OF MINE CALLED "WANDERING DETOUR" THAT I CAME UP WITH RIGHT AFTER I WON THE HOP-STEP STAR AWARD.

THE STORY IS ABOUT WHAT HAPPENS WHEN AN ELEMENTARY SCHOOL KID NAMED AKIRA AND HIS FRIENDS KATCHIN AND KAORU FIND A WALLET ON THE WAY HOME FROM SCHOOL, AND OF ALL OF THE TROUBLE THAT ENSUES WHEN THE THREE OF THEM DECIDE TO KEEP THE MONEY THAT THEY FIND AND SPEND IT ON THEMSELVES. MAYBE IT WAS TOO HARD TO FOLLOW, OR SIMPLY TOO DOWN-TO-EARTH FOR A BOYS' ADVENTURE MAGAZINE... BUT FOR WHATEVER REASON, IT WAS SUMMARILY REJECTED.

IT WAS MY FIRST REJECTION EVER. BUT I WAS SUCH A KID BACK THEN, EVEN GETTING MY FIRST REJECTION SEEMED LIKE A BIG DEAL, ANOTHER PROFESSIONAL MILESTONE I'D PASSED. FOR THE LONGEST TIME, I'D BEEN READING OTHER MANGA CARTOONISTS' TALES OF WOE ABOUT THE REJECTIONS THEY'D GOTTEN, AND I'D BEEN FEELING A LITTLE LEFT OUT. WITH "WANDERING DETOUR," I WAS FINALLY IN THE CLUB! I EVEN BRAGGED ABOUT IT A LITTLE. LIKE I SAID, I WAS A KID THEN. NOW, I'M A TRUE PROFESSIONAL, AND I AGREE WITH MY FRIENDS: "REJECTION SUCKS!" (LAUGHTER)

Number 29:
Someone Precious To You

MASTER ZABUZA...

Y-YOU'RE... THE KID I MET THIS MORNING...!!
...

WHY DID YOU STOP?
...

I MURDERED YOUR COMRADE... YOUR BELOVED FRIEND...

... AND YOU STILL SPARE ME?!

ALL THE POWER YOU HAD BEFORE... WHERE IS IT? YOU CAN'T HOPE TO KILL ME WITH THE MEAGER FORCE YOU PUT INTO THAT BLOW.
SHF
!

...DO YOU HAVE... ANYONE SPECIAL IN YOUR LIFE?
I'M WILLING TO DO WHATEVER IT TAKES... TO PROTECT THE ONE I CARE ABOUT MOST....
DOING SO IS MY OWN DREAM.
HUFF

OFTEN PEOPLE HAVE IT WRONG, MISTAKENLY BELIEVING...
... THAT SHOWING MERCY TO AN ENEMY IS KINDNESS.
THEY SPARE THE FOE WHOSE LIFE IS IN THEIR HANDS...

BUT DON'T YOU SEE?

IT'S AN EMPTY EXISTENCE...
SHA
...TO GO ON LIVING... ALONE AND UNLOVED... WHEN DEFEAT'S ALREADY COST YOU YOUR DREAM!

YOU'VE TAKEN AWAY MY REASON FOR LIVING!
HEH
MASTER ZABUZA HAS NO USE FOR A WEAK SHINOBI.

SAY WHAT?!

THAT MERCENARY SCUMBAG DOESN'T CARE WHO HE WORKS FOR OR WHO GETS HURT, JUST SO SOMEONE PAYS HIM!
WHY WASTE ALL THAT DEVOTION ON SUCH A CREEP?!

WHY...
WHEN PEOPLE ARE PROTECTING SOMETHING TRULY PRECIOUS TO THEM, THEY TRULY CAN BECOME... AS STRONG AS THEY MUST BE!
!!

...

IS THAT BROWLESS WONDER REALLY PRECIOUS TO YOU? YOUR BELOVED FRIEND?!!!

...
ONCE... I WAS PRECIOUS. I BELONGED... TO...
!
MY...
...

...PARENTS.

!
...

I WAS BORN IN A SNOWY, LITTLE VILLAGE IN THE LAND OF MIST.
AND I WAS HAPPY... MY PARENTS WERE GOOD, KIND PEOPLE.

BUT...

JUST AS I WAS GETTING OLD ENOUGH TO REALLY NOTICE THE WORLD AROUND ME...
...SOMETHING HAPPENED.

...LIKE WHAT...?
WHAT HAPPENED?

...
BLOOD. MY BLOOD.

...BLOOD...?!

...

SO...
WHAT ARE YOU TALKING ABOUT?!

MY FATHER KILLED MY MOTHER...
...AND TRIED TO KILL ME.

WHY--?

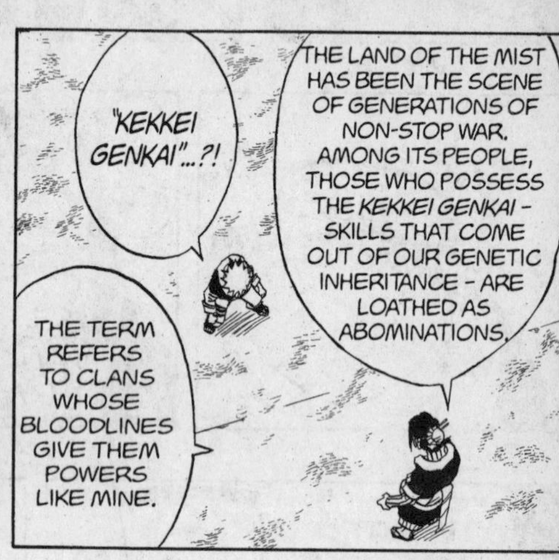
THE LAND OF THE MIST HAS BEEN THE SCENE OF GENERATIONS OF NON-STOP WAR. AMONG ITS PEOPLE, THOSE WHO POSSESS THE *KEKKEI GENKAI* - SKILLS THAT COME OUT OF OUR GENETIC INHERITANCE - ARE LOATHED AS ABOMINATIONS.
"*KEKKEI GENKAI*"...?!
THE TERM REFERS TO CLANS WHOSE BLOODLINES GIVE THEM POWERS LIKE MINE.

INHERITED SKILLS THAT WERE EXPLOITED AND TWISTED, USED TO CAUSE HORRIBLE SLAUGHTER...
...UNTIL WE CEASED TO BE LOOKED ON AS WARRIORS OR EVEN WEAPONS, BUT WERE CONDEMNED AS THE HARBINGERS OF DOOM.

AFTER THE WARS WERE OVER, WE WHO POSSESSED THIS TRAIT WERE HUNTED, ONLY ABLE TO SURVIVE BY HIDING THE EXISTENCE OF OUR SKILLS AND OUR BLOODLINE AWAY.
EXPOSURE MEANT CERTAIN DEATH!

I'M SURE THE BOY I KILLED, WHO SHARED THAT SKILL, MUST ALSO HAVE GROWN UP KNOWING THE PAIN OF WHICH I SPEAK.
WE ARE SPECIAL. WE ARE POWERFUL. AND WE ARE FEARED.

MY FATHER LEARNED... THAT MY MOTHER...
...CAME FROM SUCH A CLAN... AND BEFORE I EVEN REALIZED WHAT I WAS ABOUT TO DO...
MY FATHER HAD DIED... BY MY HAND.

...
THAT WAS THE MOST PAINFUL THING...
AND I WAS FORCED TO ACCEPT IT.

I KNEW WHAT I WAS.
AND THEN IT CAME TO ME.

SUPERFLUOUS. UNWANTED. SHUNNED.
ACCEPTING THAT I WAS ALONE IN THE WORLD.

THE MOST PAINFUL THING...?

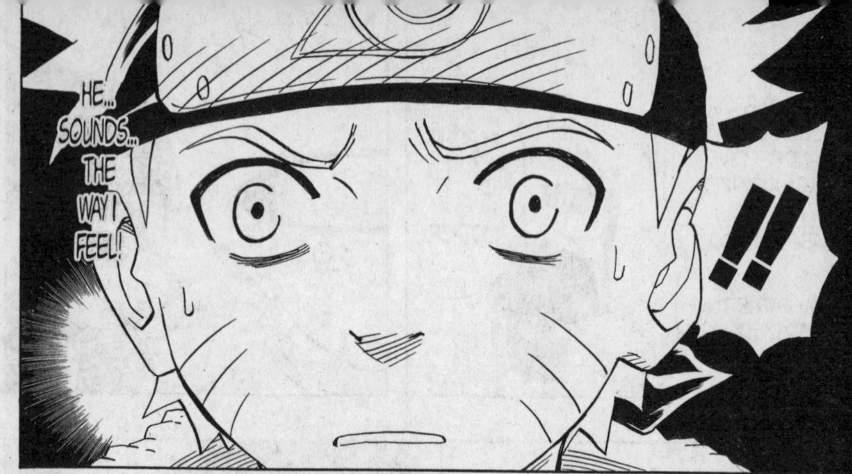
!!
HE... SOUNDS... THE WAY I FEEL!

DIDN'T YOU TELL ME...
THAT YOU WANTED TO BECOME THE NUMBER ONE NINJA IN YOUR VILLAGE AND MAKE EVERYONE RESPECT YOU?
IF YOU HAD SOMEONE IN YOUR LIFE WHO DID MORE THAN THAT... WHO ACKNOWLEDGED YOUR EXISTENCE - EVEN CARED FOR YOU --
-- WOULDN'T THAT PERSON BECOME THE MOST IMPORTANT... TREASURED... PERSON IN YOUR LIFE?!

...MASTER ZABUZA ADOPTED ME, KNOWING I CAME FROM A KEKKEI GENKAI BLOODLINE.
THE VERY THING IN ME THAT MADE EVERYONE ELSE HATE ME - HE DIDN'T JUST OVERLOOK IT. HE CHERISHED IT. HE WANTED IT!

FROM THIS DAY ON, YOU BELONG TO ME, BODY, SOUL... AND BLOOD!
COME!
!!
I WAS SO HAPPY...!!
I HAVE BAD NEWS FOR YOU, HAKU... I'M LEAVING THIS LAND TONIGHT!
BUT...! I'VE SWORN AN OATH TO RETURN ONE DAY... AS A CONQUERER, WHO'LL CRUSH THEM ALL BENEATH MY FEET!
AND TO DO THAT, WHAT I NEED FROM YOU IS NEITHER LOVE NOR AFFECTION AND SUPPORT. WHAT I REQUIRE IS...!
I UNDER-STAND.

I AM YOUR WEAPON AND YOUR TOOL.

KEEP ME BESIDE YOU, AND I'LL STRIKE WHERE YOU TELL ME TO STRIKE, KILL WHOM YOU TELL ME TO KILL.

SWUP
SWUP
SWUP
SWUP
SHINOBI CONJURATION!
EARTH STYLE! FANGED VENGEANCE TECHNIQUE!

THIS POSTURING WILL GET YOU NOWHERE, KAKASHI!
YOU CAN'T EVEN TELL WHERE I TRULY AM!!!

YOU ARE COMPLETELY ENMESHED IN MY SPELL!
WHILE I, ON THE OTHER HAND, KNOW EXACTLY WHERE YOU ARE AND EXACTLY HOW TO DEFEAT YOU!!!

!!

ONGONGONG
EH--?!

NO!!!!!
FOOM

WSH
KRAK
SNARF
SNAP
!!!
GRAB
WH-WHAT ARE WE HEARING?
!
WHEN YOUR EYES AND YOUR EARS HAVE LET YOU DOWN...
...YOU CAN ALWAYS FOLLOW YOUR NOSE!

UHN...

IT WORKED BECAUSE YOU SHUT YOUR EYES IN THE MIST.
THIS CONJURATION IS SPECIFICALLY DESIGNED FOR TRACKING.

IT'S WHY I WENT OUT OF MY WAY TO BLEED A BIT DURING BOTH OF OUR EARLIER ENCOUNTERS.
...MY LITTLE NINJA PUPS COULDN'T MISS IT!
UHN...
THE SMELL OF MY BLOOD IS ALL OVER YOU AND YOUR WEAPONS, SO THICK...

EVERY DOG HAS HIS NOSE... AND THEY ALL KNOW **YOU STINK.**
SO... WHO'S ENMESHED IN WHOSE SPELL NOW?
UGH...

THE FOG IS LIFTING. I CAN SEE YOUR FUTURE...
YOUR FUTURE IS DEATH.

KISHIMOTO MASASHI'S SECOND MANGA REJECT SPECIAL.

THE DESIGN TO THE LEFT IS FROM ANOTHER FLOP—A MANGA CALLED "ASIAN PUNK" THAT WAS RESOUNDINGLY REJECTED AT EVERY TURN. TO BE FRANK, THE PREMISE WAS—NOT COINCIDENTALLY—KINDA LIKE *GHOSTBUSTERS*.

THE MAIN CHARACTER WAS A KID WITH AN AXE TAKING ON AN EVIL FENG-SHUI MASTER WHO COULD SUMMON AND CONTROL EVIL SPIRITS... AND THE MAIN CHARACTER WASN'T REALLY HUMAN HIMSELF, BUT HAD BEEN CREATED BY SOME GREATER POWER. THERE WAS MORE, BUT WE DON'T NEED TO GO INTO IT HERE.

THE THING IS, WITH THAT STORY, MY PRIZE-WINNING SERIES *KARAKUR*, AND *NARUTO*, IT OCCURS TO ME THAT MY HEROES ARE ALWAYS THESE YOUNG GUYS. I GUESS I'M JUST A SUCKER FOR BOYS' ADVENTURE TALES!

Number 30: Your Future is...!!

YOU SAY MY FUTURE IS DEATH...?
I'VE HAD ENOUGH OF YOUR BLUFFS.

WHO'S BLUFFING NOW?
THERE'S NO WAY OUT. FACE IT.
YOU'RE GOING TO DIE.

ZABUZA...
YOU'VE HAD YOUR FUN.

...

YOU SCHEMED YOUR SCHEMES...

THE DAY YOU DESERTED THE LAND OF THE MIST AND BECAME A TURNCOAT AND RENEGADE, YOUR NAME AND YOUR ACTIONS WERE REPORTED TO US AT KONOHA VILLAGE.

WE KNOW ALL ABOUT THE FAILED COUP YOU AND YOUR FOLLOWERS STAGED, AND ABOUT THE ATTEMPT TO ASSASSINATE MIZUKAGE, THE WATER SHADOW, LEADER OF YOUR PEOPLE.

YOU'VE BEEN TRYING TO RAISE FUNDS FOR A SECOND ATTEMPT, AND BARELY STAYING A JUMP AHEAD OF THE SHINOBI HUNTERS... WHICH IS WHAT BROUGHT YOU HERE.
IT'S WHY YOU'D STOOP TO WORK FOR A PARASITE LIKE GATŌ.

FWUP

FWUP

FWUP

RRRRRM

RRRRRM

LIGHTNING BLADE!

!!
WH-WHAT THE!!

SIZZLE
I CAN ALMOST SEE... THE CHAKRA IN HIS PALM...!
YOU'RE A LOOSE CANNON...

THE MAN YOU'RE TRYING TO KILL, MR. TAZUNA, IS THE HEART AND SPIRIT OF THIS PLACE.
AND THE BRIDGE YOU'RE TRYING TO PREVENT HIM FROM COMPLETING IS THE LAND'S HOPE.

YOU'RE WILLING TO SACRIFICE THIS PLACE AND EVERYONE IN IT, JUST TO ADVANCE YOUR OWN AMBITIONS.

THAT'S NOT WHAT A TRUE SHINOBI DOES.

SPARE ME THE CIVICS LESSON AND PHILOSOPHY. I'M FIGHTING FOR MY OWN IDEALS.
AND I'M NOT ABOUT TO STOP.

I'LL SAY THIS JUST ONCE MORE.

HUH?!
GIVE UP...

YOUR FUTURE IS DEATH.

PLEASE, NARUTO. KILL ME. NOW.

WHAT ARE YOU WAITING FOR?

!

GASP!

WHAT IS WITH YOU? YOU'RE USED TO BEING THE TOUGHEST. YOU DON'T LIKE TO LOSE. I GET THAT!
BUT WANTING TO DIE JUST 'CAUSE SOMEONE BEAT YOU IS CRAZY!!

...

THERE'S MORE TO LIFE THAN JUST FIGHTING. THERE'S MORE TO YOU!

YOUR BOSS MUST LIKE YOU FOR MORE THAN JUST THAT... RIGHT? DOESN'T HE?

...
THAT DAY I MET YOU IN THE FOREST... I REMEMBER THINKING THAT WE WERE TWO OF A KIND...
SURELY YOU CAN UNDER-STAND...

!

YOU'LL HAVE TO BLOODY YOUR HANDS. FORGIVE ME FOR THAT.

IS THAT...
IS THAT THE ONLY WAY? NO OTHER OUTCOME?

YES...!!

...

...

SKRRK

...HE...
...SASUKE HAD A DREAM, TOO...

IF WE'D MET SOME OTHER WAY, SOMEPLACE ELSE, YOU AND ME'D PROBABLY HAVE BEEN FRIENDS.
CLENCH

TAK

THANK YOU.
YOU'RE GOING TO BE VERY STRONG.

THAT SUPER-THICK MIST... IT'S STARTING TO DISSIPATE...
HUH...
BUT IT LOOKS LIKE THEY'RE JUST STANDING THERE, GLARING AT EACH OTHER...
I SEE TWO PEOPLE.
!

ONE OF THEM'S MOVING!!
!!
OH!!
IT'S HARD TO MAKE OUT...
WHICH ONE IS YOUR MASTER KAKASHI?

RRRRROAR!!

!!

HUNH?!

I'M SORRY, NARUTO!

!!!
WHAT?
KLATTER
DRIP
DRIP
DRIP
plit
plit
plit

!!
SCHUUULGKK
AIEE!!
WH-WHAT THE-!!

SPLAT
SPLATTER

POOF

!

KOFF
!

ZABUZA... S-SIR...
!

...YOU SAID MY FUTURE WAS DEATH...
HEH HEH... BUT YOU MISSED AGAIN, KAKASHI.
SNEER

Number 31:
To Each His Own Struggle...
夢

BAM
BAM BAM

MISTER GI'ICHI!
BAM BAM
OPEN UP! PLEASE!!!
BAM

PUFF
PUFF
I NEED YOU TO COME WITH ME TO THE BRIDGE!!!
IF WE STICK TOGETHER, THIS TIME WE CAN BEAT GATô AND HIS WHOLE GANG!

I'M SORRY... INARI, WE'RE NOT GOING TO FIGHT BACK ANY MORE...

!
YOUR FATHER...
..WAS A HERO. BUT HE'S GONE NOW.

IF WE FIGHT, WE'LL BE THROWING AWAY A LOT OF LIVES.
WE'VE ALREADY SACRIFICED AND LOST SO MUCH.
NONE OF US WANTS ANY MORE LOSSES... ANY MORE REGRETS.

...
...I DON'T WANT ANY REGRETS EITHER.

THAT'S WHY...
...I HAVE TO FIGHT.

...

A MAN HAS TO LIVE HIS LIFE SO THAT HE DOESN'T END UP WITH ANY REGRETS...

...I LOVE MY MA, AND GRANDPA, AND YOU...
...AND EVERY-ONE IN THE VILLAGE...

...

AND I UNDERSTAND NOW...
THAT I CAN'T PROTECT ANYONE BY BEING A BIG CRYBABY.
SKF
TAK
...
LITTLE INARI IS GROWING UP TO BE A FINE YOUNG MAN, ISN'T HE...
ARE YOU SURE HE'LL BE ALL RIGHT LIKE THAT... BY HIMSELF?

YOU'RE JUST A LITTLE BOY!
TROMP
TROMP

I MAY BE LITTLE...
... BUT I KNOW HOW TO FIGHT...

'CAUSE I'M MY DADDY'S SON.
...

INARI, WAIT!
KREEEEAK

!

HAKU...
WHERE IS HE?!
FWP
FWP

!
THE MIST'S FADING... I'M SEEING THINGS MORE CLEARLY...

HUNH?!

TAK
IS THAT HIM?!

!!
PUFF
HUFF
HUFF

WH-...
WHAT... WHAT IN...?!

SCHLUUGK

ISN'T THAT THAT BOY IN THE MASK...?!

CLENCH

HE JUMPED BETWEEN... TO SAVE ZABUZA...

...

HEH HEH...
...

THAT WAS BRILLIANT... HAKU.

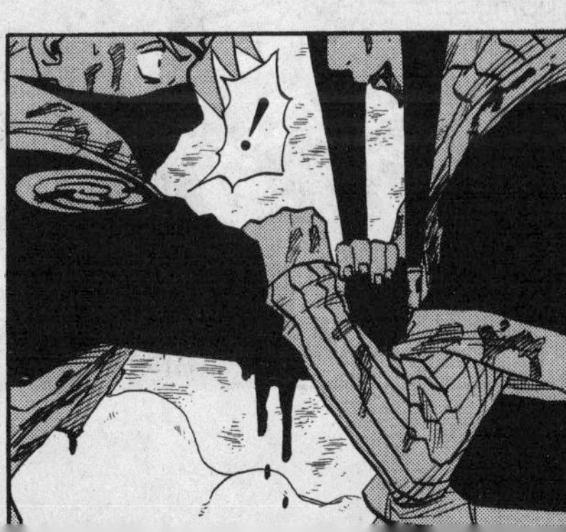
!

...THE BOY...

...IS ALREADY...

...DEAD.

!!
MASTER KAKASHI!!
I AM YOUR WEAPON AND YOUR TOOL...
I REALLY DID FIND A TREASURE IN THAT GUTTER...
TO THINK THAT HE'D GRANT ME THIS MARVELOUS CHANCE IN THE END!!
ARRRH--!
GRAB

THAT UNFORGIVABLE SCUMBAG!
GRRR

HEH HEH... SO...YOU WERE ABLE TO GET AWAY... BECAUSE POOR HAKU WAS ALREADY DEAD.

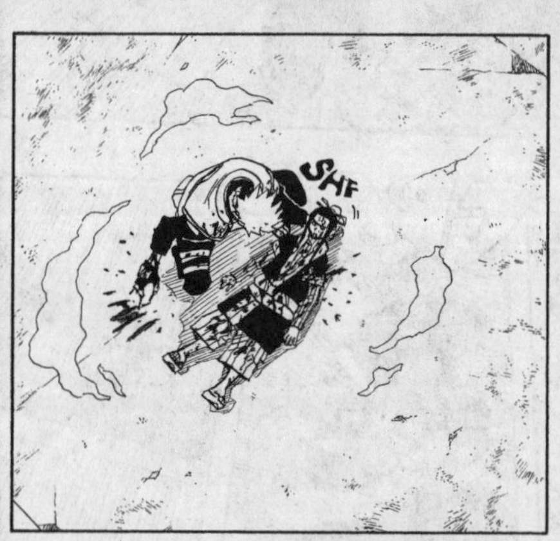
SHF

NARUTO... STAY OUT OF THIS!
!

...NARUTO...?

!

THIS IS MY FIGHT!!

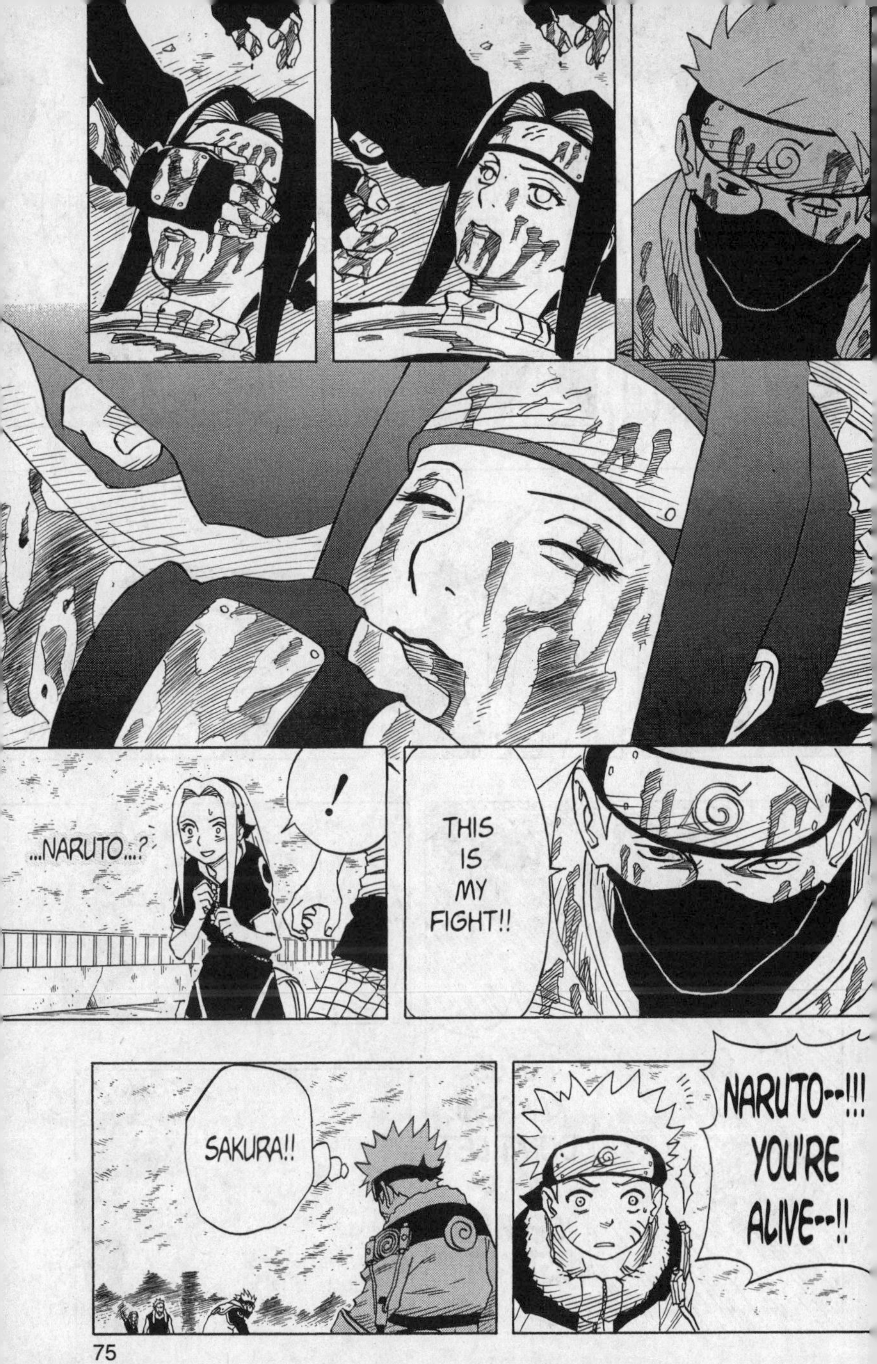

SAKURA!!

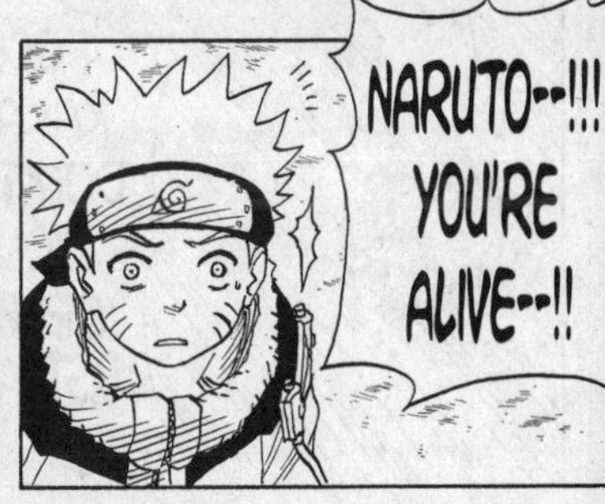
NARUTO--!!! YOU'RE ALIVE--!!

HUH?
WHAT ABOUT SASUKE?

NARUTO!! WHERE'S SASUKE?!!!
!!
FLINCH

...

?

...

...

TAK
FOCUS, KAKASHI! DON'T LET YOUR-SELF BE DISTRACTED!!!
!!

GACK

!
TREMMBLE

...I'LL STAY WITH YOU
SO THAT YOU WON'T BE DISOBEYING YOUR MASTER'S ORDER.

...
GRIP
UH-HUHN.

TAK

!!

SKFF

SHA

HE'S SO COLD.
THIS ISN'T AN ILLUSION... IS IT...?

DON'T HOLD BACK FOR MY SAKE. THERE ARE TIMES WHEN IT'S RIGHT TO GIVE IN AND SHED SOME GOOD HONEST TEARS.

I...
... ALWAYS GOT PERFECT SCORES ON ALL MY TESTS IN SCHOOL.

!

I MEMORIZED EACH AND EVERY ONE OF THE ONE HUNDRED RULES OF CONDUCT FOR NINJA AND SHINOBI. I USED TO WRITE THEM OUT WITH PRIDE.
WE HAD A TEST ONE DAY. AND THE QUESTION WAS ...

...!

"WHAT IS THE TWENTY-FIFTH RULE OF SHINOBI CONDUCT?"
JUST LIKE ALWAYS, I WROTE IT DOWN.

?!

"NO MATTER WHAT HAPPENS, TRUE SHINOBI MUST NEVER... EVER... SHOW THEIR EMOTIONS!

"TH-THE MISSION IS THE ONLY PRIORITY. CARRY THAT IN YOUR HEART. AND NEVER, NEVER, SH-SHED A TEAR..."

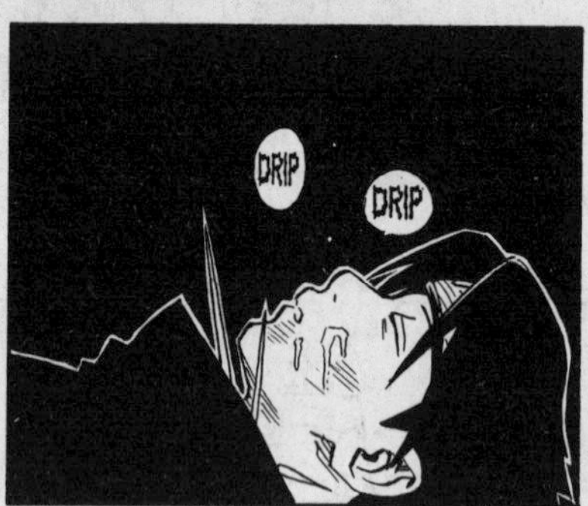

SO THIS... THIS IS WHAT A SHINOBI IS... IT'S UNBEARABLE...
SASUKE...!!

WHY... WHY... CAN'T I KEEP UP...?
HUFF
HUFF
HUFF
HUFF

DAMN IT!!
TAK

WHOP

...!

UHN...!

SHHF
GRAB
!!

WH
A

IT'S OVER. YOU JUST DON'T KNOW IT YET.

NOW THERE'S NO WAY YOU CAN BEAT ME.
WHAT?!

TAP

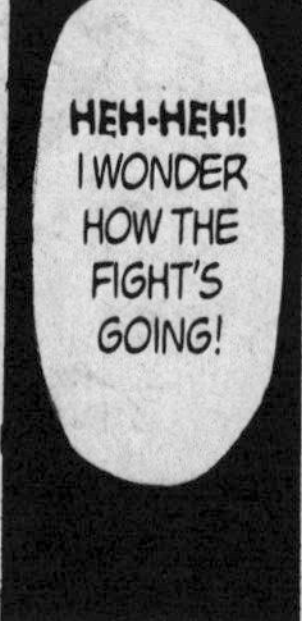
HEH-HEH! I WONDER HOW THE FIGHT'S GOING!

FWUP

FWUP

!!

SMAK

32: THE TOOLS CALLED SHINOBI

THIS IS GOOD-BYE...
..."DEMON"!
SHUKK

!

!!
Number 32:
The Tools Called Shinobi

KOFF
DRIP
!
K-KLUNK

BABAM
ZABUZA!
MUTTER
GATŌ...
WHAT ARE YOU... DOING HERE? AND... WHY.... DID YOU... BRING... ALL OF THEM?!
HIM...
HEH HEH HEH— THERE'S BEEN A SLIGHT CHANGE OF PLAN, ZABUZA. OR OF YOUR PLANS, ANYWAY.
—THIS WAS WHAT I HAD IN MIND ALL ALONG.

YOU'RE GOING TO DIE, "DEMON"... HERE AND NOW.
WHAT?
YOU MUST HAVE GUESSED. I NEVER INTENDED TO PAY YOU.

...IT'S SUCH A BOTHER HIRING A SKILLED SHINOBI AFFILIATED WITH ONE OF THE TOP VILLAGES. IT'S EXPENSIVE... AND THEY TEND TO HAVE FRIENDS WHO OBJECT WHEN I BETRAY AND KILL THEM.
IT'S SO MUCH SIMPLER TO HIRE *NUKENIN*— RENEGADES— LIKE YOURSELF. NO ONE CARES WHAT I DO TO YOUR KIND ONCE THE JOB IS DONE.
ALL OF YOU NINJA ARE SO EAGER TO FIGHT EACH OTHER. ONCE YOU'VE WORN EACH OTHER DOWN, COMMON THUGS CAN FINISH OFF THE REST.
IT'S A GREAT BUSINESS PLAN— EFFICIENT AND INEXPENSIVE.

MY ONLY MISTAKE WAS HIRING YOU IN THE FIRST PLACE.
CALLING YOURSELF THE DEMON OF KIRIGAKURE IS JUST PLAIN FALSE ADVERTISING!
HEH HEH... YOU'RE NO DEMON...
MORE LIKE A **BABY** DEMON, IF THAT.

GAHAHAHAHAHAHA!
THE SHAPE YOU'RE IN, WE'LL TAKE YOU DOWN WITHOUT EVEN BREAKING A SWEAT!

HAHAHAHAHA
WHO ARE THEY?
THAT'S SOME CROWD!

HA HAHA
FORGIVE ME... KAKASHI...
OUR FIGHT IS OVER.
GYAH
!!

I NO LONGER HAVE ANY REASON TO WANT TO ASSASSINATE TAZUNA...
...WHICH SETTLES OUR DIFFERENCES.

HA HAHA
YEAH...
HUH?

GYAHAHA
YOU'RE RIGHT.
HA HA HA HA

...THAT REMINDS ME...
!
!
TAP TAP
TOK

I STILL HAVE A SCORE TO SETTLE.
AAARGH!!

TAP
TAP

YOU... CRUSHED MY ARM UNTIL YOU ALMOST BROKE THE BONES!
POKE

HAH.
DEAD MEAT. CARRION.
KICK

WHAT ARE YOU DOING, YOU CREEP?!

DASH

COOL DOWN. THINK. THERE'S A LOT OF THEM.
HEY!!
GRAB

HEY, WHY DON'T YOU DO SOMETHING?! HE WORKED FOR YOU! HE WAS PRACTICALLY YOUR SLAVE!!

LIKE WHAT?
HAKU IS DEAD.
!!
BUT...
BUT YOU SHOULD CARE! THAT FAT SCUMBAG IS DESECRATING HIM!!!
HE WAS YOUR COMRADE... YOUR PARTNER... HE WORKED FOR YOU FOR YEARS!!!
...GATō'S BEEN USING ME... AND I USED HAKU.
WEREN'T YOU LISTENING? IT'S A SHINOBI'S LOT. ALL OF US ARE EITHER USERS, OR TOOLS... OR BOTH.
I DIDN'T VALUE HAKU FOR HIMSELF... BUT FOR THE TAINT HIS BLOOD CARRIED... AND FOR WHAT HIS TALENTS COULD DO FOR ME.
I APOLOGIZE FOR NOTHING.
YOU...
DO YOU REALLY MEAN THAT?
...
!
CHFF
STOP IT, NARUTO! LEAVE HIM ALONE. OUR QUARREL IS OVER.
BESIDES WHICH...

SHUT UP--!!

HE'S STILL MY ENEMY!!!

-HUFF-

-HUFF-

-HUFF-

...

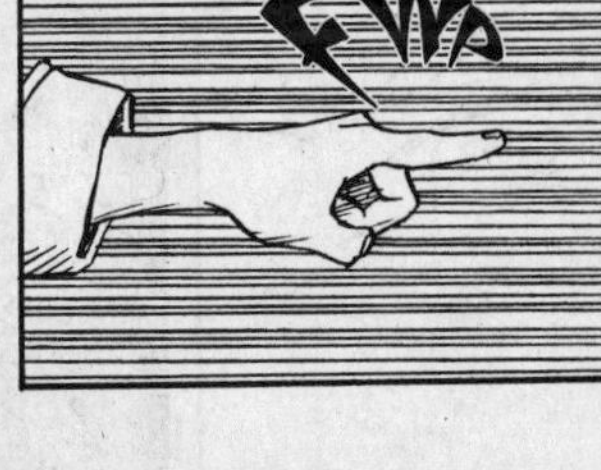

DO YOU HAVE ANYONE SPECIAL IN YOUR LIFE?
HE WAS DEVOTED TO YOU!!

WHEN PEOPLE ARE PROTECTING SOMETHING TRULY PRECIOUS TO THEM...
...THEY TRULY CAN BECOME... AS STRONG AS THEY MUST BE!

...

BUT YOU THINK THAT'S JUST NOTHING, THAT HE WAS NOTHING. YOU DON'T FEEL A THING!

I...FIND IT DIFFICULT TO EMBRACE THE FULL SHINOBI PHILOSOPHY.

ARE YOU REALLY THAT HEARTLESS?

I'M WILLING TO DO WHATEVER IT TAKES... TO FULFILL THAT PERSON'S DREAMS...
TO THAT END, I WILL BECOME A TRUE SHINOBI...

IS THAT HOW YOU GET... WHEN YOUR POWERS ARE AS STRONG AS YOURS ARE?

HE GAVE HIS LIFE FOR YOU!

I'M WILLING TO DO WHATEVER IT TAKES... TO FULFILL THAT PERSON'S DREAMS...
DOING SO IS MY OWN DREAM.

HE DIED... WITHOUT ANY OF HIS DREAMS EVER COMING TRUE.

I WAS SO HAPPY...!

TO DIE AS HIS TOOL...

THAT'S... TOO MUCH, TOO CRUEL...

...
KID.
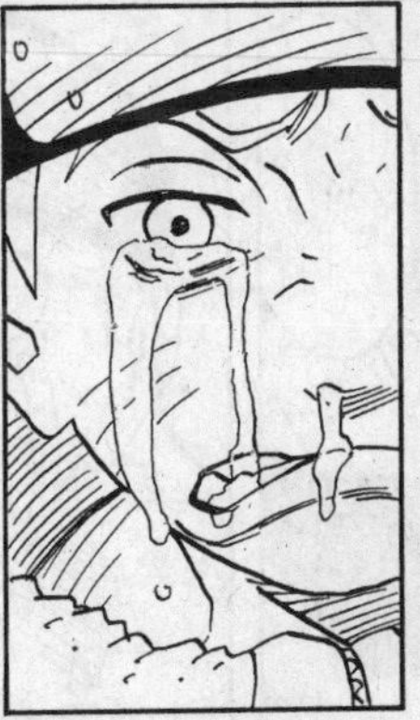

PLIT
PLIT

...NOT...

...ANOTHER WORD.

PLIT

PLIT

KID...

...!
GHA

WHAT HAKU DID... WAS NOT JUST FOR ME.
WHILE WE FOUGHT, HE BROKE HIS HEART... OVER YOU... AND YOUR FRIENDS. THAT'S THE TRUTH.

BITE
SHARRRED
HE WAS TOO KIND... TOO GENTLE.

?!
...I'M GLAD MY LAST BATTLE... WAS AGAINST YOU...BOY.
YOU'RE RIGHT, YOU KNOW.
...HUH?

!
SAY WHAT WE WILL, DO WHAT WE WILL. IN THE END, WE SHINOBI ARE STILL JUST PEOPLE AFTER ALL... WITH FEELINGS ALL-TOO-HUMAN.
AND I'VE LOST... EVERYTHING.

...
FLUTTER
WOULD YOU LEND ME YOUR KUNAI KNIFE?

!!
HUNH? UH...
SURE.

CHUCK!

WHAT?!

THOP

TIK

THAT'S ENOUGH! WHAT ARE YOU WAITING FOR? KILL ALL OF THEM!

THOP

THOP

YEAH!!

TOK TOK TOK

LET'S GO!

YOU DON'T STAND A CHANCE!

EVEN IF YOU'RE A NINJA, YOU'RE HALF-DEAD, AGAINST ALL OF US!

A...
A DEMON!!

!

CHOK CHOK CHOK
WHY WON'T YOU DIE?!
CHUKKK

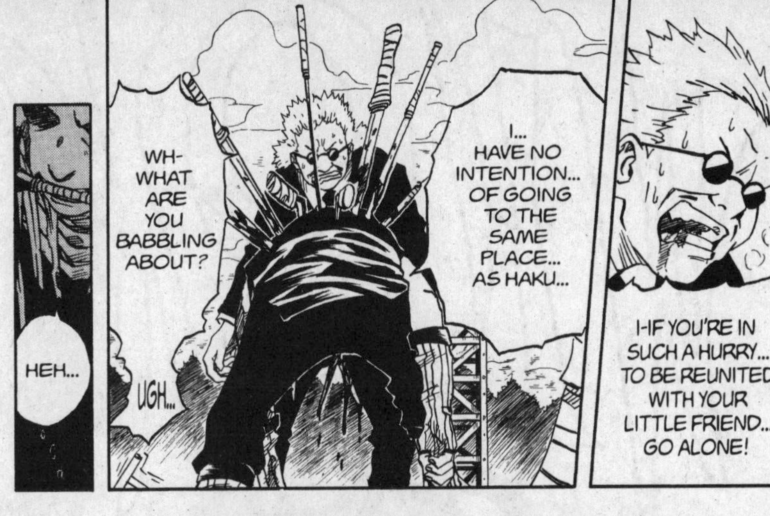
I-IF YOU'RE IN SUCH A HURRY... TO BE REUNITED WITH YOUR LITTLE FRIEND... GO ALONE!
I... HAVE NO INTENTION... OF GOING TO THE SAME PLACE... AS HAKU...
WH- WHAT ARE YOU BABBLING ABOUT?
UGH...
HEH...

...I'M TAKING YOU WITH ME...
...TO HELL!!

EVEN AN OGRE IN NAME ONLY... A WASHOUT FROM KIRIGAKURE VILLAGE... CAN BECOME A REAL DEMON IN HOW HE MEETS HIS DEATH.

AHH--!

SPLURT

AIEEE--!

ONCE WE'RE IN HELL, I CAN TAKE MY TIME, AND SHOW YOU OVER... AND OVER... WHO IS, OR IS NOT, "A BABY DEMON"!

!!

SHUFF

WHOK
AUUGH!!
THOP
THOP
THUD
GULP
...

GRRR
RRR

EEEEK!!

STUMBLE

PLEASE... KEEP ME BESIDE YOU...

IT'S... GOODBYE NOW, HAKU...
THANKS FOR EVERYTHING...
AND I'M SORRY...

KISHIMOTO MASASHI'S THIRD MANGA REJECT SPECIAL!

ONCE AGAIN, THE ROUGH SKETCH TO THE LEFT IS FROM ANOTHER REJECTED MANGA. IT WAS A BASEBALL MANGA, TITLED SIMPLY "BASEBALL KING." I PLAYED BASEBALL MYSELF, BACK IN MY STUDENT DAYS, SO I (MAYBE FOOLISHLY) THOUGHT I WOULD TRY MY HAND AT A BASEBALL STORY.

DURING THIS PERIOD, I WAS IN A SITUATION WHERE, NO MATTER HOW MANY CONCEPTS FOR ADVENTURE MANGA I SKETCHED OUT, I DIDN'T GET ANY GREEN LIGHTS, SO I THOUGHT I SHOULD GO FOR A SPORTS THEME.

BUT WHEN I ACTUALLY TRIED TO DRAW ONE, PERHAPS BECAUSE I WAS WRITING FROM PERSONAL EXPERIENCE, IT BECAME A MORE REALISTIC WORK THAN I HAD INTENDED.

THE REASON IT FAILED WAS THAT IT WAS TOO SERIOUS FOR A SHONEN PUBLICATION. IT WASN'T ENTERTAINMENT.

HOWEVER, "BASEBALL KING" ACTUALLY STILL HOLDS A SPECIAL PLACE IN MY HEART. I SOMETIMES FIND MYSELF THINKING, "THAT WAS SO FUNNY... I CAN'T BELIEVE IT'S A REJECT, DARN IT...!"

33: HERO'S BRIDGE!!
DON'T LOOK AWAY.
THIS WAS THE END OF A MAN WHO LIVED FULL OUT.
...
YEAH...
SOB
SASUKE...
LUB-DUP
SOB
SOB
AM I... DEAD...?
SOB
SOB
AM I... AM I...?!
SAKURA...?!
SOB

Number 33: Hero's Bridge!!
...SAKURA...
YOUR ARM'S HEAVY...

SHUDDER
...!!

...?

SNIFF
SOB
DRIP
DRIP
SNIFF

SASUKE!!!!
SASUKE!
SASUKE!!
GRAB
!

OHHHH!!

I'M SO HAPPY FOR YOU, SAKURA.

SAKURA... YOU'RE HURTING ME...
OH!
S-SORRY...

...

OOF

!!

...I'M ALL RIGHT... HOW'S NARUTO?

AND THAT... LITTLE CREEP IN THE MASK... WHAT HAPPENED TO HIM?

DON'T TRY TO MOVE!

NARUTO'S FINE! AND THE BOY IN THE MASK IS DEAD...

DID NARUTO...?
DEAD--?!
N-NO...
I MEAN... I'M NOT SURE. I DIDN'T SEE IT VERY WELL. BUT THE BOY DIED TRYING TO PROTECT ZABUZA.

I... WAS AFRAID.... I THOUGHT...

YOU'RE AMAZING, SASUKE. YOU SURVIVED A DEATHBLOW.
I'M SO GLAD...

NOT ME. HIM.

...HE NEVER PLANNED TO... FROM THE START...

!
NARUTO--!!
SAKURA?!!
HUNH?

IT'S SASUKE. HE'S ALL RIGHT!!
HE'S ALIVE!!

--!!

...

...

...

HEH... HEH...

I GET IT... HE....

HAKU ....WHILE WE FOUGHT, HE BROKE HIS HEART... OVER YOU... AND YOUR FRIENDS. THAT'S THE TRUTH.
HE WAS TOO KIND... TOO GENTLE.

I'VE BEEN WORRYING SINCE THE FIGHT BEGAN... BUT...
SASUKE MADE IT AFTER ALL. FANTASTIC!

SASUKE!!

HEY!
RATTLE
THOP
AREN'T YOU SWEET-HEARTS FORGETTING SOMETHING?!

!
!!

YOU NINJA KILLED OUR MEAL TICKET!
AND NOW YOU'RE GONNA DIE!!!
THE ONLY WAY WE CAN EVEN BREAK EVEN NOW...
...IS TO OVERRUN THE CITY AND LOOT EVERY BUSINESS AND HOME!!
OH YEAH!
K-CHK
K-CHK
CHAAAARGE
LET'S GO!
UHHH... THIS ISN'T GOOD.
MASTER KAKASHI-ISN'T THERE SOME TECHNIQUE WE CAN USE TO TAKE THEM ALL DOWN AT ONCE?
I'M AFRAID... WITH THE LIGHTNING BLADE, THE ILLUSIONS AND CONJURATIONS... FOR THE MOMENT, I'VE EXHAUSTED MY CHAKRA.
SHOOP
!!
HEYY--!
SKID
STEP
STUMBLE
THUKK
!?

STOP WHERE YOU ARE.
THIS ISLAND IS OUR HOME. ONE STEP FURTHER...
YOU'LL DIE WHERE YOU STAND!
...
INARI...
ALL OF YOU...
INARI!!
HEH HEH.
IT'S BEING A HERO, YOU KNOW? ALL THAT NICK OF TIME STUFF!

ONWNG

ART OF THE SHADOW DOPPLE-GANGER!!
FWUP
FLIP
GOOD ONE, KID. MIND IF I JOIN IN?

BUT A BLUFF SHOULD BE ENOUGH FOR THESE BOZOS!
FWUP

I CAN'T MANAGE ANYTHING SOLID WITH MY CHAKRA SO LOW.

YIPE!

ART OF THE SHADOW DOPPLE-GANGER!!
KAKASHI STYLE

TAK TAKTAKTAK
NEVER MIND!!
RUN AWAY!!!

YAY..!!
OO-HOO!!!

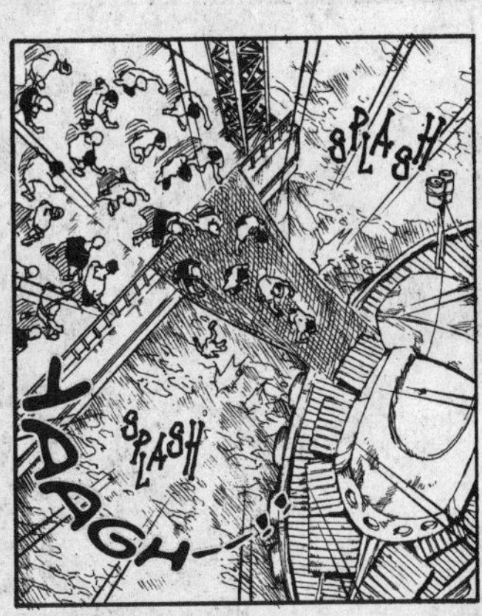
SPLASH
SPLASH
YAAAGH--

SKF

POOF
POOF
POOF

...LOOKS LIKE IT'S ALL OVER...
...EH, KAKASHI?
YEAH.

KAKASHI... DO ME A FAVOR?

WHAT IS IT?

...I WANT TO...
...SEE... HIS FACE.

...

YANK
SURE.

CHF

HUH?

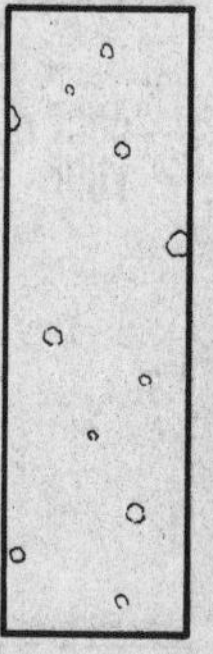

...
IT'S SNOWING.

ARE YOU CRYING?
MY DEAR HAKU...

IN THE MIDDLE OF SUMMER...?

...THANK YOU ... KAKASHI.

YOU WERE AT MY SIDE RIGHT FROM THE START...
AND I'M AT YOURS, NOW, AT THE END...

...IF I COULD... ...IF I WERE ABLE... I WOULD WANT TO GO... TO THE SAME PLACE... ON THE OTHER SIDE ...
...AS YOU.

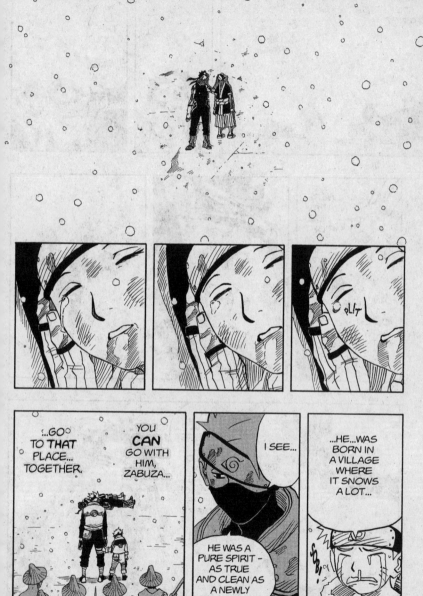

PLIT

YOU CAN GO WITH HIM, ZABUZA...
...GO TO THAT PLACE... TOGETHER.

I SEE...
HE WAS A PURE SPIRIT - AS TRUE AND CLEAN AS A NEWLY FALLEN SNOW.

...HE...WAS BORN IN A VILLAGE WHERE IT SNOWS A LOT...
SOB!

TWO WEEKS LATER

GRAB

HACK
OWW!

WHAT SNEAKY, GREEDY TRICK ARE YOU UP TO NOW?
GRRR
HEH HEH
YOU EAT AN OFFERING, YOU'LL BE PUNISHED BY THE GODS!

...
BUT STILL...
MASTER KAKASHI...

HMM--?

...I CAN'T HELP WONDERING. WERE THOSE TWO RIGHT ABOUT WHAT A NINJA SHOULD BE?

A *SHINOBI* SHOULDN'T BE CONCERNED WITH A REASON FOR HER OWN EXISTENCE...
IT IS IMPORTANT MERELY THAT WE EXIST AS A TOOL FOR OUR HOMELAND TO USE IN WHATEVER WAY THEY NEED.
THAT'S AS TRUE FOR US IN KONOHAGAKURE AS IT FOR NINJA ANYWHERE ELSE.
...

IS THAT REALLY WHAT BECOMING A FULL-FLEDGED NINJA'S GONNA BE ABOUT?
I DON'T LIKE THE SOUND OF IT!

DO YOU REALLY FEEL THAT WAY, MASTER KAKASHI?
WELLL... NO.
AND THAT'S WHY ALL WE NINJA LIVE OUR LIVES WITH THAT IDEAL ALWAYS BUBBLING BENEATH THE SURFACE OF OUR MINDS, DISTURBING US.
...LIKE IT DID ZABUZA...
AND THE BOY...
...
THAT'S IT. I'VE MADE UP MY MIND!
I AM GOING TO CREATE MY OWN NINDO— MY OWN NINJA PATH. MY OWN DESTINY!
!

THANKS TO YOU, OUR BRIDGE HAS FINALLY BEEN COMPLETED, BUT...
IT'S GOING TO BE AWFULLY DULL AROUND HERE, ONCE YOU'RE GONE.

WE'VE ENJOYED YOUR HOSPITALITY.
NO PROBLEMO, TAZUNA, MY MAN!! WE'LL COME BACK TO PLAY WITH YOU AGAIN SOMETIME!

PAT
YOU BETTER...
TREMBLE
...AW...

LUB-DUP
SO... UM... ANYWAY...
...
INARI... DON'T LET IT GET YOU DOWN.
IT'S OKAY TO CRY, IF YOU REALLY WANT!
TREMBLE
...

I'M NOT GONNA CRY!!
B-BUT NARUTO... HEY, "BIG BROTHER" ... Y-YOU CAN CRY! GO AHEAD!

ME? NO WAY.
FWUP
SEE YOU.
SKUFF

OH!

BLUBBER
KIDS!
SOB!

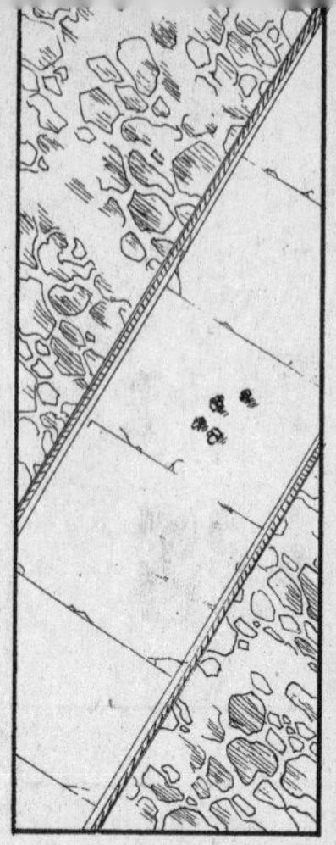

THAT BOY TOUCHED LITTLE INARI'S HEART... AND INARI TOUCHED THE HEARTS OF ALL THE PEOPLE IN OUR CITY...
NARUTO BUILT THE BRIDGE THAT EVENTUALLY CARRIED US ALL TO HOPE AND COURAGE!

AND SPEAKING OF BRIDGES, WE STILL HAVE TO OFFICIALLY DEDICATE THIS ONE.
AND THERE'S ONLY ONE NAME THAT WILL TRULY FIT.

WHAT ARE WE GOING TO CALL IT?

HOW ABOUT... THE GREAT NARUTO BRIDGE?

HEE HEE... IT'S A NICE NAME.

ALL RIGHT--! LET'S GET HOME. MASTER IRUKA'S GONNA TAKE ME OUT FOR RAMEN NOODLES TO CELEBRATE US ACCOMPLISHING OUR MISSION!

AND THEN... AND THEN, YOU KNOW, I HAVE TO TELL LITTLE KONOHAMARU MY EPIC TALE OF MARTIAL ARTS BRAVERY--!!

OH... UH... OKAY. BY THE WAY, SASUKE... WHEN WE DO GET HOME... WOULD YOU LIKE TO... GO OUT WITH ME?

UH, NO. THANKS.

N-NO...?...

HEY! **I'LL** GO OUT WITH YOU!

NARUTO! NO! KNOCK IT OFF!

ARE YOU SURE? CALLING IT THAT...?!
HEH... QUITE SURE. YOU SEE, I HOPE THAT IN GIVING IT THAT NAME, WE'LL ENSURE THAT IT WILL STAND FOREVER...

OUR BRIDGE WILL BECOME SUPER-FAMOUS THE WORLD OVER, AS A SYMBOL OF TRIUMPH AND ENDURANCE!
THAT'S WHAT I HOPE... AND HOPEFULLY, THAT'S HOW IT'LL BE.

Number 34: Intruders?
忍
縁招
木葉茶通り

YAAAAAWN

MILK
RAMEN

野菜をたべよう
MUNCH
MUNCH

GLUG GLUG

POK

HEH

TAK
WOO-HOO! NO MATTER WHAT TODAY'S MISSION IS, I'LL HAVE THE ENERGY TO FACE IT NOW!
START YOUR ENGINES!! MACH 5!!

OH!
GOOD MORNING, SAKURAAAA!!

!
SKID
!

...
...
SKF

...
HMMF!

NOT AGAIN!
EVER SINCE WE GOT HOME FROM THE LAND OF WAVES, THESE TWO HAVE BEEN ACTING JUST PLAIN WEIRD!
IT'S SOOO EMBARRASSING!
?
DIE, FREAKS!
INNER SAKURA
ANY TIME NOW, MASTER KAKASHI! HURRY UUUUP!!

...

THREE HOURS LATER..

GOOD MORNING, EVERYONE.

I'M AFRAID I GOT LOST ON THE WAY HERE...

YOUR NOSE IS GROWING, MASTER!!!

YOU ALWAYS LAY IT ON TOO THICK.

AS NINJA DECEPTIONS GO... THAT ONE SUCKS!

HEY, MASTER KAKASHI! ANY HOT NEW MISSIONS FOR THE 7TH CELL? WE'VE HAD NOTHING BUT GIMMES! BORRRRING!

SIZZLE

WE WANT ACTION! A CHALLENGE! SOMETHING WHERE I COULD USE MY SKILL -LIKE THIS... AND THIS... AND - AND -

OH, REALLY?

I SEE WHERE YOU'RE GOING WITH THIS...

HEY, NARUTO! WAKE UP! WE'RE HEADING OUT ON OUR MISSION!

YESSIR!

WOULD YOU CHILL?!

OPENS TODAY
AT LAST IT COMES TO LIFE!
MAKE-OUT PARADISE
AND AT THE MISSION'S END...
SIGH...
THROB
THROB
YOU'D HAVE BEEN FINE IF YOU HADN'T OVERDONE IT.
YOU'RE A REAL NUISANCE.

SNAP
!
FLINCH

THAT DOES IT!! SASUKE...
IF YOU START ANYTHING MORE, I'LL BURY YOU!
...
HAH!

HMM...
LATELY... YOUR TEAMWORK HAS BEEN ALMOST NON-EXISTENT.

YOU TELL HIM! YOU'RE ALWAYS MESSING UP OUR TEAMWORK, SASUKE!!
HE WAS TALKING TO YOU, PINHEAD.
IF YOU'RE SO SICK OF BEING IN MY DEBT...

WHY DON'T YOU...
GET BETTER THAN ME?

!!

I DON'T KNOW HOW THEY MANAGED IT, BUT THEY'RE ON EVEN WORSE TERMS NOW THAN THEY WERE BEFORE.

I HATE THIS... THERE ARE GUYS OUT THERE WHO COULD CHALLENGE ME, BUT I'M STUCK ON NOTHING ASSIGNMENTS WITH THIS TWERP.
BITE

SKREE
SKREE

!
BOP
FLIP

OKAY, THAT'S IT. WE'LL CALL IT A DAY RIGHT NOW.
I'VE GOT TO GO HAND IN MY REPORT ON TODAY'S MISSION.
THEN I'M GOING HOME.
SHHHF

!
OH!

HEY! SASUKE, WAIT UP!
...
I... I WAS WONDERING... IF... ♡

AW, MAN!!!

IF WE, YOU KNOW... YOU AND I... JUST THE TWO OF US... COULD WORK ON OUR, UM... OUR ♡ TEAMWORK?
YOU'RE AS BAD AS NARUTO.

WHY WASTE YOUR TIME FLIRTING WHEN YOU SHOULD BE PRACTICING?
LIKE NARUTO!
INNER SAKURA
THUNK

EVEN HIS SKILLS ARE BETTER THAN YOURS!
WORSE THAN NARUTO!
NO WAY!!!
INNER SAKURA!!
THUNK
THUD

SKF SKF

HE'S RIGHT... IT DOESN'T MATTER WHAT OUR MISSION IS. THEY'RE ALL THE SAME TO ME...
'CAUSE I'M ALWAYS THE WEAKEST... THE ONE WITH ALMOST NO SPECIAL SKILLS!

HEY, HOT STUFF! FORGET SASUKE. YOU AND I CAN TRAIN TOGETHER!
FLINCH

FWOOM

HUH?
WHERE'D MASTER KAKASHI GO? IS HE GIVING US SOME ALONE TIME?

WHATEVER! WHAT MATTERS IS, I'M DONE LOSING! THERE'S ONLY ONE THING AHEAD OF ME, AND THAT'S... TRAINING!
SNEAK
SNEAK

HUH?!
STOP!

A ROCK? WHY IS A ROCK SNEAKING UP ON ME?

FWIP
RUSTLE

LITTLE HINT... NO ROCK HAS PERFECT ANGLES, PERFECT CORNERS... AND EYE HOLES. KIND OF A BIG CLUE.
FWP
YIPE
RATTLE
OW!
PSYCH!! FAKED YOU OUT, ROCK!!!
TA-DAAAA
LEAVE IT TO THE MAN I HAVE ACKNOWLEDGED AS BEING ALMOST MY EQUAL! YOUR SKILLS RIVAL MY OWN!!
OOF
GRUNT
...
HEH HEH HEH
YOU'RE OUR IDOL, RIGHT? WE'RE COPYING THE STYLE YOU USED TO WEAR.
UHHH...
WHAT'S UP WITH THE GOGGLES?
OH, IT'S YOU GUYS.

OH-
KAAAAAY....
WHAT
DO
YOU
MEAN,
"OKAY?"
SUDDENLY
TOO
COOL
FOR
SCHOOL,
BIG
GUY?
!

WHAT
DO
YOU
WANT
FROM
ME?
WE'LL
SHOW YOU,
BOSS!
CAN YOU
COME
NOW?
HE'S LOOKING
DOWN ON US!

NOPE!
I
HAVE
TO
TRAIN!
FWUP

BUT... BUT YOU
PROMISED
TO PLAY NINJA
WITH US!!
RIGHT?
HEH...
OH,
YEAH...
WAS
THAT
TODAY?
IF I PLAY
WITH
THEM,
EVEN A
LITTLE,
THEY'LL
WASTE
MY WHOLE
DAY!

SO...
JUST
WHAT IS
A NINJA
DOING
"PLAYING
NINJA",
HMM?
DUM DUM DOM
TAK
TAK
...

UH, YES? CAN WE HELP YOU?
BUT WHO AM I TO TALK? I'M WORSE THAN HE IS!

GRR

!

THAT CHICK'S EYING HIM LIKE SHE'D LIKE TO KILL HIM AND DEVOUR HIS CORPSE!

THE WAY SHE'S LOOKING AT ME... STOP! I'M BLUSHING!!
HEY, BIG GUY, WHO'S THE BABE?

!!
JINK
...YOU KNOWWWW! RIGHT?

HEY, BIG GUY, SEEING AS HOW YOU'RE SO SMART AND SUAVE AND ALL...
BOFF
HUNH?
THE HOTTIE... I CAN TELL... YOU AND SHE ARE......

HEH HEH HEH
FOR LITTLE GUYS, YOU CATCH ON QUICK.
WRONG!!!
POW

WHOP
THUMP
SKID
BIG GUY!!
BAM

(PUFF) (HUFF) (PUFF)
WH-WHAT DID YOU DO THAT FOR?!
YOU'RE OUR LEADER! YOU CAN'T DIE!
OWWW...
YOU TOTAL WITCH!
INNER SAKURA
LEMME AT 'IM!
CRUNCH

THANKS FOR YOUR LATEST REPORT, MASTER KAKASHI.
...
HOW'S OUR LITTLE HELLION?
DOES HE GET ALONG WELL WITH THE OTHER MEMBERS OF HIS CELL?
HE'S... GETTING THERE.
YOUR TEAM'S SEEN A LOT OF ACTION LATELY.
NARUTO HASN'T HAD TIME TO GET TOGETHER WITH ME ONCE. I CAN'T HELP WORRYING ABOUT HIM.
SCRATCH
YOU KNOW HOW IT IS, MASTER IRUKA. UCHIHA SASUKE IS IN OUR CELL, TOO. HE AND NARUTO ARE LIKE A COUPLE OF DOGS, ALWAYS CIRCLING EACH OTHER, SNAPPING AND SNARLING.
BUT IT KEEPS NARUTO ON HIS TOES. HE'S DEVELOPING FAST. HE'S ALWAYS HOPING TO CATCH UP TO HIS HERO... **YOU.**
...!
REALLY?

KONOHA-MARU! ARE YOU ALL RIGHT?
Sigh
HMF
STOMP
STOMP

HUMPH!

!!
...JEESH! THAT BROAD-BROWED, FIREBREATHING HAG! IS SHE EVEN A REAL FEMALE?!
OWW

YIPE!

RUUUUUN
ARRRRRGH!!

OOOONG
THAT'S GOTTA SMART!
!!

TUHTWEEET

NOW WHAT?

!
HUFF
HUFF
HUFF

NOW'S THE TIME!

MUNCH

KONOHA-
MARU!!

UNNH...
THAT HURT, SNOTFACE!

KNOCK IT OFF. YOU'RE GONNA GET IT AS IT IS!

IT WAS MY FAULT. I WAS FOOLING AROUND...
WHO ARE THESE PEOPLE?

PUT HIM DOWN, YOU BIG APE!!

THESE GUYS MUST BE GENIN - JUNIOR-LEVEL NINJA - FROM KONOHA VILLAGE!

I JUST WANT TO PLAY WITH HIM A LITTLE... WHILE WE'RE WAITING FOR THE NUISANCE TO GET HERE!
OWW!
KRUNCH

YOU!

ZOOM

GRRR
FLIP

GAAH!!
TRIP

?
WHAT WAS THAT?!

WHAT A WIMP!
IS THAT THE BEST KONOHA'S *GENIN* CAN DO?!

TH-THEY'RE FOREIGNERS!
WHY ARE THEY HERE?

SEEING WHOM I INVITED HERE, YOU MAY BE ABLE TO GUESS...

...WHAT WE ARE HERE TO DISCUSS.

IS IT TIME ALREADY?
HAVE YOU INFORMED THE LORDS OF THE OTHER LANDS YET?
BECAUSE I BELIEVE I HAVE ALREADY SEEN SOME OF THEM IN OUR VILLAGE.
WHEN IS IT TO BE?

ONE WEEK FROM TODAY.
ISN'T THIS RATHER SUDDEN?

HUMF

TO MAKE IT COMPLETELY OFFICIAL, I HEREBY ANNOUNCE...
SEVEN DAYS FROM NOW, ON JULY 1ST...
WE SHALL BEGIN CONDUCTING EXAMINATIONS FOR JOURNEYMEN NINJA – THE *CHŪNIN*.

Number 35:
Iruka vs. Kakashi

KONOHA-MARU!!

KONOHA-MARU!!

...

HEY! YOU IN THE BLACK PIG SUIT!!
RELEASE HIM NOW AND I'LL GO EASY ON YOU, GOON!!

YOU'RE THE GOON!
CHOKE
DO YOU WANT THAT GUY TO BEAT YOU UP?!
GACK!!

YOU'RE STARTING TO ANNOY ME!
!

GUK
GASP
FIRST OFF, I'M ALLERGIC TO "SHRIMP"!
BAD ENOUGH THAT YOU'RE A SHORT LITTLE KID... YOU'RE DISRESPECTING YOUR ELDERS! YOU MAKE ME WANT TO KILL HIM!

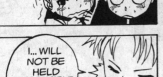

!!
WHAT?!

I... WILL NOT BE HELD RESPONSIBLE FOR THIS...

YOU-
WHO IS HE? THIS IS SO NOT GOOD!

SHHK
CRUNCH
♥ SO I'LL FINISH WITH THIS TINY SHRIMP... AND MOVE ON TO THE JUMBO SHRIMP OVER THERE.

!!

THWIP

YOU... YOU...

THOK
THO
AAGH!
UGH!
TELL ME... WHAT ARE YOU GUYS DOING IN OUR VILLAGE?
IT'S SASUKE !!
SO?
HMM... PRETTY COOL!

NOW, THEN...
WE'D LIKE TO HEAR FIRST FROM THOSE WHO HAVE OVERSEEN THE TRAINING OF OUR NEWEST JUNIOR NINJA.
TAK
MASTERS KAKASHI, KURENAI, AND ASUMA.
TELL US...
...DO ANY OF YOU HAVE, AMONG YOUR CHARGES, ANY *GENIN* YOU'D RECOMMEND FOR THIS YEAR'S JOURNEYMEN EXAMS?

...THAT BEFORE WE CAN EVEN CONSIDER THEM,
THEY MUST HAVE COMPLETED A MINIMUM OF EIGHT MISSIONS.

BEYOND THAT, EMPLOY YOUR OWN JUDGMENT AS TO WHETHER THEY ARE READY TO ASPIRE TO THE NEXT LEVEL.

YOU MAY BEGIN, KAKASHI.

TO BE TRULY COMPETITIVE, CANDIDATES SHOULD PROBABLY HAVE COMPLETED AT LEAST DOUBLE THE RECOMMENDED NUMBER OF MISSIONS...
HE SHOULDN'T BE ASKING THIS YET.... IT'S TOO SOON FOR **ANY** OF THEM.

CELL NUMBER 7, LED BY KAKASHI, CONSISTS OF UCHIHA SASUKE, UZUMAKI NARUTO, AND HARUNO SAKURA. I VOW UPON THE HONOR OF MY CLAN, THE HATAKE -

- THAT ALL THREE OF THEM ARE READY FOR THE *CHŪNIN* SELECTION EXAM.

CELL NUMBER 8, LED BY KURENAI, CONSISTS OF HYUGA HINATA, INUZUKA KIBA, AND ABURAME SHINO. I VOW UPON MY OWN CLAN, THE YUHI, THAT I AM AS CERTAIN AS IS MY ESTEEMED COLLEAGUE -
- THAT ALL THREE ARE READY FOR THE *CHÛNIN* SELECTION EXAM.

WHAT?!

HOW UNUSUAL FOR ALL THREE OF YOU TO HAVE UNHESITATINGLY ASSENTED...

CELL NUMBER 10, LED BY ASUMA, CONSISTS OF YAMANAKA INO, NARA SHIKAMARU, AND AKIMICHI CHOJI. I VOW UPON MY CLAN, THE SARUTOBI, THAT I AM EQUALLY AS CERTAIN -
- THAT ALL THREE ARE READY FOR THE *CHÛNIN* SELECTION EXAM.

LORD HOKAGE!
PLEASE ALLOW ME TO SPEAK!!

YES, IRUKA?

J-JUST A MOMENT!!

FORGIVE ME IF I OVERSTEP, BUT MOST OF THE NINE STUDENTS JUST NAMED...
... WERE MY STUDENTS WHILE THEY WERE AT THE ACADEMY.
CERTAINLY, THEY ARE ALL GIFTED AND SHOW BOTH COMMITMENT AND TALENT... BUT IT'S TOO SOON FOR KIDS THAT YOUNG TO BE STEPPING UP TO THE JOURNEYMAN LEVEL.

NARUTO'S NOT LIKE YOU!

I WAS SIX YEARS YOUNGER THAN NARUTO WHEN I ATTAINED THE RANK OF *CHŪNIN*, IRUKA.

ONLY WITH TIME WILL THEY HAVE THE KIND OF EXPERIENCE AND MATURITY THOSE EXAMS REQUIRE.
I DON'T UNDERSTAND WHY THEIR SUPERVISORS CAN'T SEE THAT.

THEY GRIPE ABOUT EVERY DETAIL OF EVERY MISSION. JUST FOR ONCE, I THINK IT WOULD DO THEM GOOD TO FIND OUT WHAT REAL PAIN IS...
LET'S ADMIT IT. BREAKING THEM WOULD BE FUN.
ARE YOU OUT OF YOUR MIND?

YOU ALL KNOW WHAT THEY CALL THE *CHŪNIN* SELECTION EXAMS, DON'T YOU?
DO YOU WANT TO DESTROY THOSE CHILDREN?!

...IT WAS A JOKE, MASTER IRUKA.
I UNDERSTAND YOU... AND I'M SORRY IF MY RECOMMENDATION UPSETS YOU. BUT I STAND BY IT.
BUT...
KAKASHI... CAN WE FINISH WITH THIS?
IT'S NONE OF YOUR BUSINESS, ANYWAY...
...THEY'RE NOT YOUR STUDENTS ANYMORE.
THEY ARE SOLDIERS UNDER MY COMMAND.
...
WHAT A PEST.
...
火

TAK

OH, LOOK. ANOTHER LITTLE BRAT.

GET LOST.

OOO... HOW COOL!!

NARUTO.... YOU SUCK!
I CAN'T BELIEVE WE LOOKED UP TO YOU!

DON'T BE STUPID. I COULD HAVE HANDLED THAT LOSER IF SASUKE HADN'T BUTTED IN!
RIIIGHT.

HE DID IT AGAIN - STICKING HIS NOSE IN AND MAKING ME LOOK BAD!!

COME DOWN, LITTLE SQUIRREL!

THINK YOU'RE PRETTY SMART, DON'T YOU?
SHF

TELL ME YOU'RE NOT PLANNING TO USE THE 'CROW!
FWIP
TOK

KANKURO! DON'T!
!!

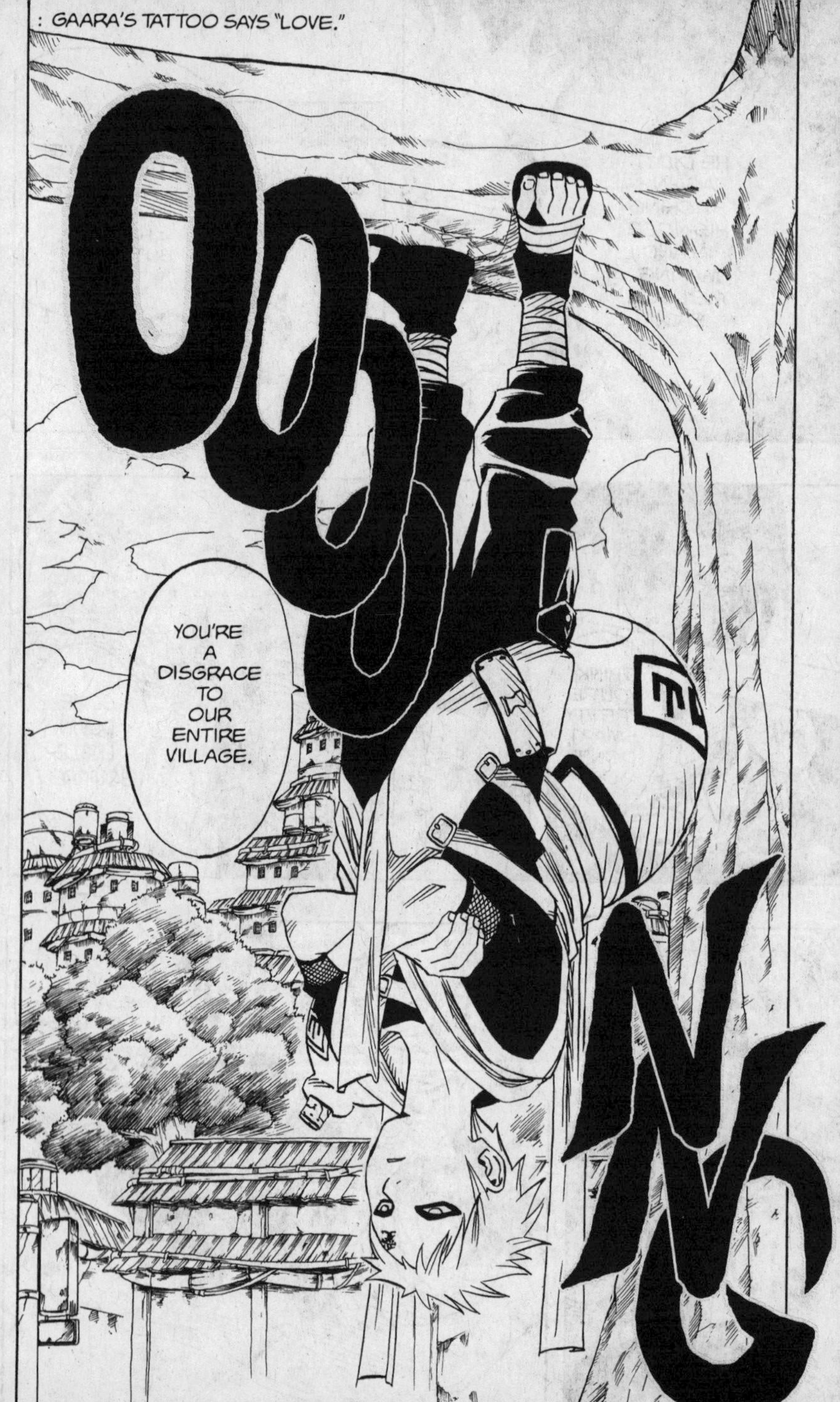
: GAARA'S TATTOO SAYS "LOVE."
YOU'RE A DISGRACE TO OUR ENTIRE VILLAGE.

G-
GAA-
RA...

HE...
HE SNUCK UP BESIDE ME...
I DIDN'T EVEN HAVE A CLUE!

HIS STEALTH SKILLS RIVAL KAKASHI'S.

IT ANNOYS ME THAT YOU'D LOSE CONTROL IN A QUARREL WITH CHILDREN!
HAVE YOU FORGOTTEN WHY WE CAME HERE?

BUT GAARA... THEY STARTED IT. THE LITTLE ONE SLAMMED ME!

SHUT UP...

OR I'LL KILL YOU.

SHIVER

YOU'RE RIGHT. I WAS OUT OF LINE.
WE'RE SORRY... OKAY, GAARA?
REALLY. REALLY SORRY!

SO HE'S IN CHARGE, EH?
HE GLARES LIKE A BASILISK.
SORRY ABOUT MY FRIENDS.

!!
FWP

THIS IS THE ONE WHO NAILED KANKURO WITH A STONE. THAT TOOK SKILL.

!
I KNOW WE'RE A LITTLE EARLY...
SHHM
... BUT WE DIDN'T COME HERE TO PLAY AROUND.
I SWEAR IT WON'T HAPPEN AGAIN.

LET'S GO.
WAIT!
!

YES?
ACCORDING TO YOUR HEADBANDS, YOU THREE...
...COME FROM THE VILLAGE HIDDEN IN THE SAND.

YOUR COUNTRY IS ONE OF KONOHA'S ALLIES...
...BUT ACCORDING TO OUR TREATY, YOUR NINJA ARE NOT PERMITTED TO CROSS THE BORDER WITHOUT AUTHORIZATION.

STATE YOUR BUSINESS!
WE CAN'T JUST LET YOU GO YOUR MERRY WAY.

...EVER HEARD THE OLD SAYING ABOUT IT BEING DARKEST AT THE BASE OF THE BRIGHTEST LIGHT-HOUSE?
TA-DA! MY TRAVEL PAPERS!
WEREN'T YOU INFORMED?

!

AS YOU GUESSED, WE'RE JUNIOR-LEVEL NINJA FROM THE HIDDEN SAND VILLAGE.
WE'RE HERE TO TAKE THE *CHŪNIN* SELECTION EXAM

...
WHAT'S THE *CHŪNIN* SELECTION EXAM?

YOU REALLY DON'T KNOW? JUNIOR NINJA ARE SENT FROM THE HIDDEN SAND VILLAGE AND THE MINOR LANDS BETWEEN OUR HOME AND YOURS TO COMPETE AGAINST KONOHA'S OWN CANDIDATES.
WHY TEST US ALL TOGETHER?
MAINLY TO MAINTAIN THE SKILL OF ALL SHINOBI AT THE SAME HIGH LEVEL OF EXCELLENCE. ALSO TO FOSTER FRIENDSHIP AND UNDERSTANDING BETWEEN NINJA. AND, OF COURSE, TO MAINTAIN THE BALANCE OF POWER BETWEEN THE LANDS THEMSELVES.

HEY, KONOHAMARU! MAYBE I SHOULD ENTER THIS CHÛNIN SELECTION EXAM THING TOO, HUH?
LISTEN, YOU! WHEN YOU ASK SOMEONE A QUESTION, IT'S CONSIDERED GOOD MANNERS TO LISTEN TO THEIR ENTIRE ANSWER.
FUMM

HEY! YOU THERE! WHAT'S YOUR NAME?
POP

HUH?

W-WHO, ME?

NO!

I WAS TALKING TO THE SPOOK BESIDE YOU.

...

!

!

...

GAARA OF THE DESERT, AT YOUR SERVICE.

AND YOU ARE...?

!

UCHIHA SASUKE.

HEH

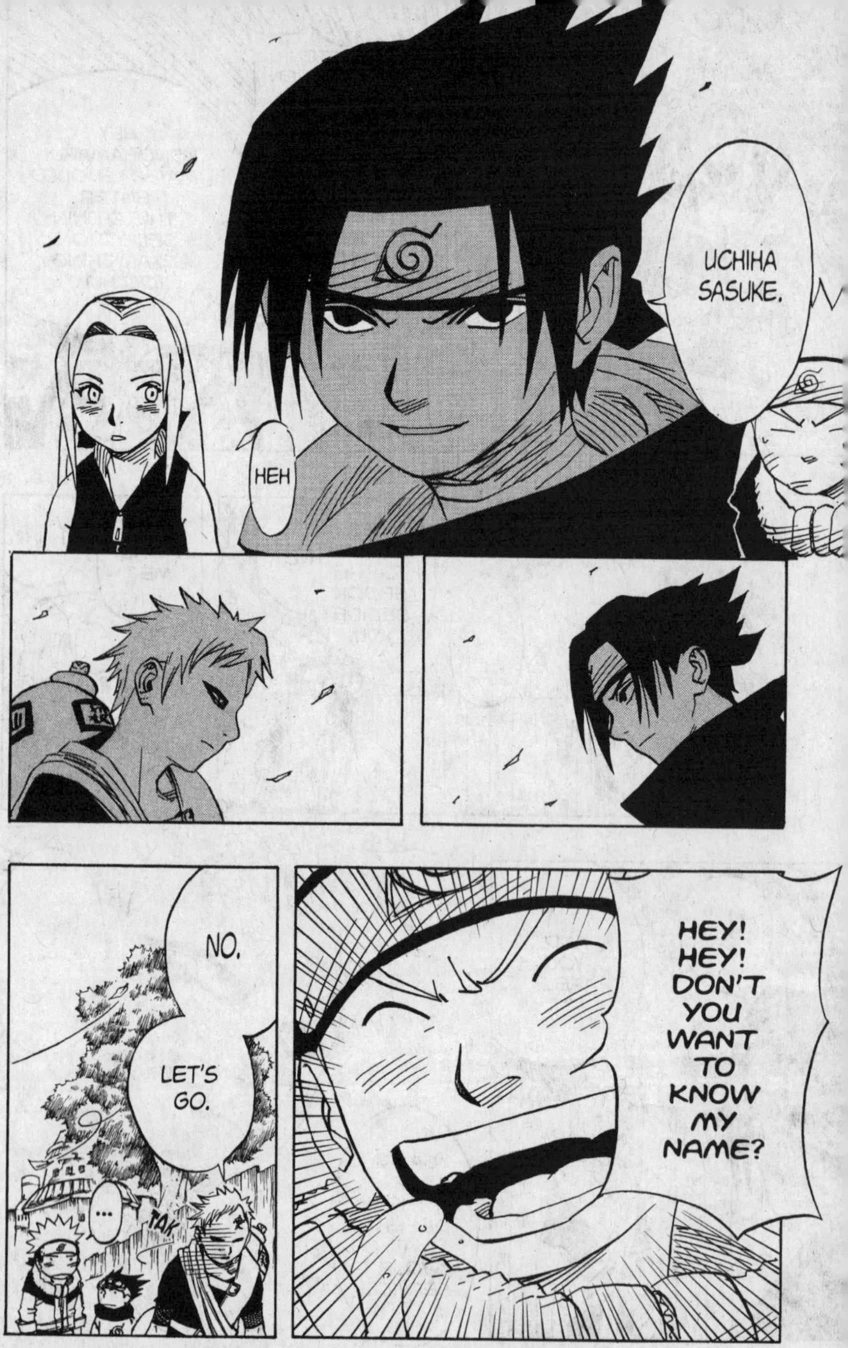

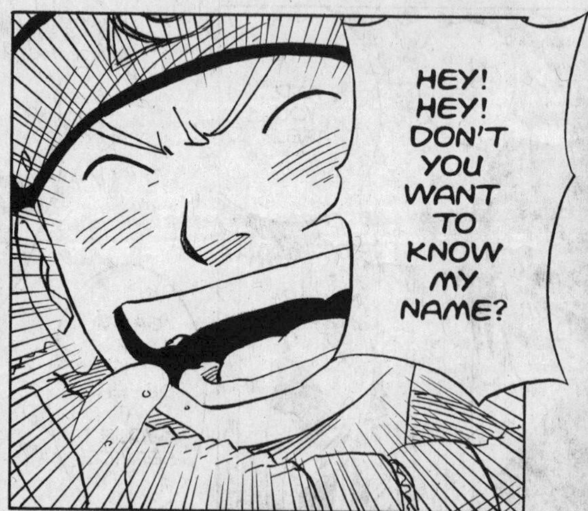

HEY! HEY! DON'T YOU WANT TO KNOW MY NAME?

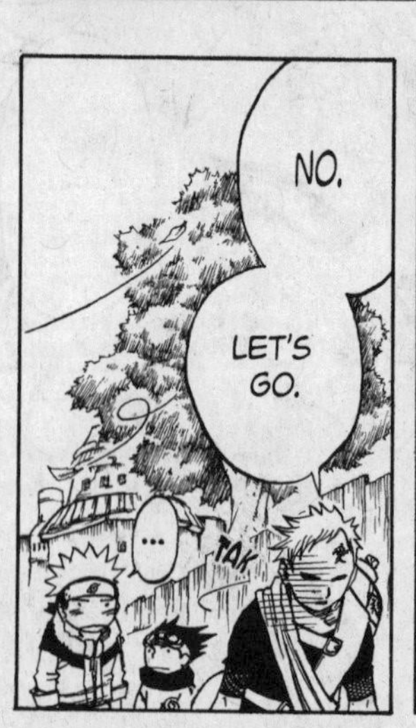

THINGS ARE GETTING INTERESTING.
KONOHA-MARU, DO I LOOK LIKE SUCH A LOSER?
NEXT TO SASUKE, BIG GUY... YEAH.
SNIFF

SASUKE!! I AIN'T GONNA TAKE THIS!

WHERE DO YOU GET OFF STICKING YOUR NOSE IN?

WHAT DO YOU THINK?

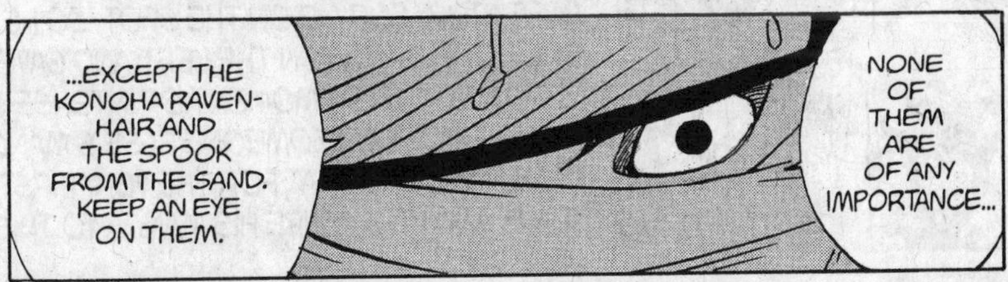

NONE OF THEM ARE OF ANY IMPORTANCE...
...EXCEPT THE KONOHA RAVEN-HAIR AND THE SPOOK FROM THE SAND. KEEP AN EYE ON THEM.

KISHIMOTO MASASHI'S

THE END

POINTLESS LITTLE STORY

THE EIGHT-PANEL *MANGA* ON THE LEFT BRINGS BACK FOND MEMORIES FOR ME OF KOISHI, THE FRIEND WHO DREW IT FOR ME BACK IN COLLEGE. I HAD BEEN DRAWING *MANGA* SINCE MY HIGH SCHOOL DAYS, BUT I DIDN'T HAVE A SINGLE FRIEND WHO SHARED MY PASSION. IN COLLEGE, I HEARD OF A GROUP OF MANGA FANS AND ASPIRING ARTISTS WHO CALLED THEMSELVES THE *MANKEN*, OR MANGA LAB. BUT THEY WEREN'T SO MUCH DRAWING MANGA AS THEY WERE PATTING EACH OTHER ON THE BACK FOR DRAWING PINUPS AND ILLUSTRATIONS WITH NO ATTEMPT AT STORYTELLING WHATSOEVER. I AVOIDED THOSE PHONIES LIKE THE PLAGUE AND WENT MY OWN WAY, TRYING TO DRAW ACTUAL MANGA.

THEN, ONE DAY, I MET A MAN WHO CLAIMED HE HAD DRAWN AUTHENTIC *MANGA* BACK IN HIGH SCHOOL. I HAD DOUBTS ABOUT WHETHER HE WAS ON THE LEVEL, SO I CHALLENGED HIM. I WAS DETERMINED TO FIND OUT WHETHER HE WAS A REAL MANGA ARTIST OR ANOTHER PHONY. I DEMANDED THAT HE DRAW A TWO-PAGE STORY FOR ME ON THE SPOT. SO HE DREW THE MANGA ON THE LEFT AND GAVE IT TO ME. IT WAS A MOMENT OF INTENSE JOY FOR ME TO HOLD SOMEONE ELSE'S MANGA IN MY HAND LIKE THAT, FOR THE VERY FIRST TIME, AND I TREASURE HIS MANGA TO THIS VERY DAY.

HEY! HEY! HEY, DID YOU HEAR?
36: SAKURA'S DEPRESSION

THE *CHÛNIN* EXAM'S COMING UP... WORD IS THEY'LL BE LETTING MEMBERS OF THE ROOKIE CLASS COMPETE FOR THE FIRST TIME IN FIVE YEARS!
NO WAY!
IT PROBABLY HAS SOMETHING TO DO WITH THE RIVALRY AMONG THE *JÔNIN* ELITE.
TWIRL TWIRL

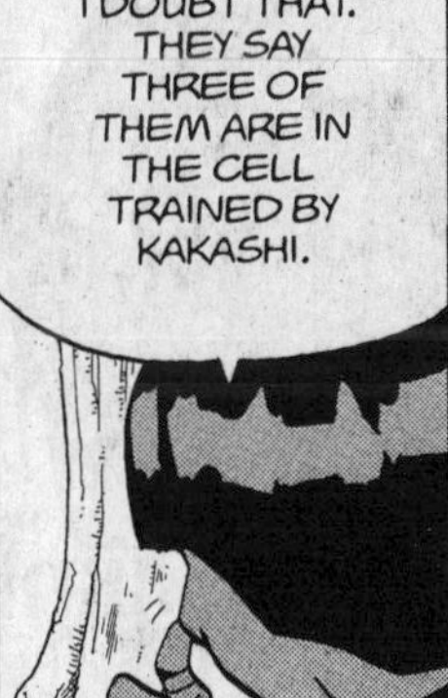
I DOUBT THAT. THEY SAY THREE OF THEM ARE IN THE CELL TRAINED BY KAKASHI.

THE KAKASHI? THAT'S INTERESTING...
POK

FWP
WELL, EITHER WAY—

THU

IT ALL HAS A VERY SAD SOUND TO IT.
Number 36:
Sakura's Depression

SLUMP
SHEESH!
SIGH

I MEAN, THINK HOW I FEEL. I OVERSLEPT, AND I DIDN'T EVEN GET TO BLOW-DRY MY HAIR!
SHE'S RIGHT! SAY IT, SAKURA!!
WE ⇨ CAN TELL
YEAH

OKAY, LOOK! ARE WE GOING TO JUST STAND AROUND AND LET THEM GET AWAY WITH THIS?
WHY IS IT, WHENEVER WE GET CALLED OUT, WE END UP WAITING LIKE DOPES FOR THE CHALLENGER TO SHOW?

WHY DO THESE TWO ALWAYS WAKE UP FEELING DRAMATIC?
EWWW! GROSS!
HEH...
RRRR
GRRR GRRR

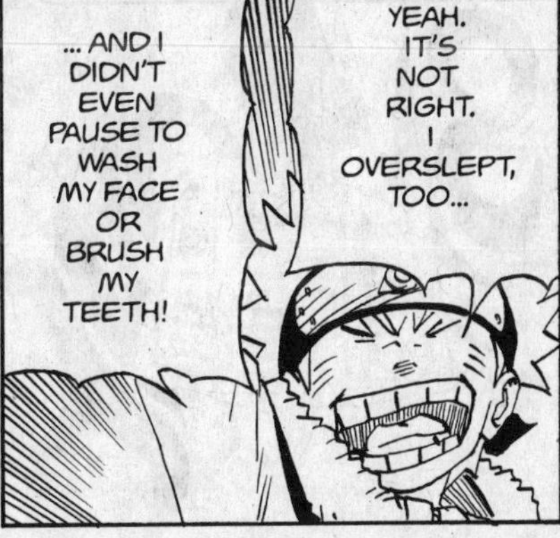
YEAH. IT'S NOT RIGHT. I OVERSLEPT, TOO...
... AND I DIDN'T EVEN PAUSE TO WASH MY FACE OR BRUSH MY TEETH!

MORNING, GUYS!!
TODAY, I WANDERED A BIT FROM THE PATH OF LIFE...
!!
YOU ARE SUCH A LIAR!!
WOULD IT KILL YOU TO AT LEAST PRETEND TO BE SORRY?
IN ANY CASE...

THIS MAY SURPRISE YOU...
BUT I'VE RECOMMENDED ALL THREE OF YOU FOR THE *CHÛNIN* SELECTION EXAM.
DOOOONNNN

HUH?!
...
!

SAY WHAT?!
GOOD ONE, MASTER. YOU ALMOST HAD US.
YOU HAVE TO FILL OUT APPLICATIONS.
JOURNEYMAN

HEH
HEH
HEH
HEH

...
MASTER KAKASHI, I LOVE YOU!!
GRAB
GET OFF... YOU'RE EMBARRASSING ME!

YOU NEEDN'T TURN IN THOSE APPLICATION FORMS UNLESS YOU WANT TO.
IF YOU DO, REPORT TO ROOM 301 AT THE SCHOOL BY 4:00 TOMORROW AFTERNOON.

IF ANY OF YOU DON'T WISH TO COMPETE, THE EXAM IS ENTIRELY VOLUNTARY.
THE CHOICE IS YOURS.

FWMM
THAT'S ALL!

TAK
DUM-DI-DI-DUH... THE JOURNEYMAN NINJA SELECTION EXAM!
TAK
I'LL BET THERE'LL BE A LOT OF TOUGH COMPETITION.

I SWEAR, I AM NOT GONNA LET ANYONE BEAT ME!!

!
AND THAT OTHER ONE!!
FWMM
RARRR

LIKE HIM!!
PLIT

YYYYAYYYY!
REPLACED BY NARUTO... I GUESS THE BEST MAN WON...
HEE HEE HEE!
TIME FOR THIS SENILE OLD FOOL TO RETIRE!

YA AY
IN HIS DREAMS!
IF I COULD WIN SOMETHING THIS BIG... I
PHOOEY
...IT'D BE SMOOTH SAILING TO BECOME THE NEXT LORD HOKAGE!
2

READ THIS WAY

...

I MIGHT GET TO FACE OFF AGAINST THAT SPOOK.
SHIVER

HAH!

...
LA-DI-DI-DA

...

!...
...DON'T WANT TO.

FORGET SASUKE... I CAN'T EVEN KEEP UP WITH NARUTO.
THIS EXAM WOULD BE TOO MUCH FOR ME.

THE NEXT DAY....

酒酒屋
HEY, SAKURA!
冷し中華はじめました
よろこんで!!

UH... HI.
...

WHAT'S...
UP WITH HER?
IS THIS WHERE I SIGN MY NAME?
CAN'T YOU READ?

NINJA ACADEMY
忍

RUSH
RUSH
生
欲

IS SOMEONE AS TALENTLESS AS YOU REALLY PLANNING TO TAKE THE *CHÛNIN* SELECTION EXAM?
WHY BOTHER?

BUNCH OF WET-BEHIND-THE-EARS SNOTNOSES!
SNERK
YOU SAID IT!

PLEASE... WE'RE BEGGING YOU... LET US IN.

301
TAK
TAK

301
THP

!!
UHN-

...THAT'S JUST CRUEL...!

WHAT DID YOU SAY?

YOU MISUNDERSTAND!
WE'RE JUST TRYING TO SPARE YOU...

THE *CHÛNIN* EXAM IS INCREDIBLY DIFFICULT... AND WE SHOULD KNOW. WE'VE FAILED THREE TIMES SO FAR.
THERE ARE PEOPLE WHO MADE IT, THEN IMMEDIATELY GAVE UP BEING SHINOBI... OTHERS WHO ENDED UP CRIPPLED... SOME REDUCED TO VEGETABLES... WE'VE SEEN IT ALL!

!!
WHOA
AW, MAN

BESIDES THAT, *CHÛNIN* ARE CELL COMMANDERS. THEY LEAD THEIR UNITS.
THE RESPONSIBILITIES FOR FAILED MISSIONS AND DEAD SHINOBI REST FIRMLY ON THEIR SHOULDERS.

AND YOU LITTLE PUNKS HAVE THE NERVE TO APPLY?
SNORT

WE'RE SAVING A STEP BY WEEDING OUT THE OBVIOUS LOSERS BEFOREHAND.

301
THAT SOUNDS GOOD IN THEORY...

... BUT YOU'D BETTER LET ME THROUGH.
AND DROP THE FORCE-FIELD ILLUSION YOU'VE CREATED, WHILE YOU'RE AT IT.

I HAVE BUSINESS ON THE THIRD FLOOR.
WHAT'S HE TALKING ABOUT?
WHO KNOWS?
TAK
...!

301
HEH...

SO YOU FIGURED THAT OUT, EH?

IT WAS EASY. RIGHT, SAKURA?
YOU WERE PROBABLY THE FIRST TO NOTICE IT.
HUH...?
YOU'RE THE MOST ANALYTICAL AND THE BEST IN OUR CELL...
...AT UNDERSTANDING THE ART OF ILLUSION.
WINK
...
SASUKE...
...
?
...THANK YOU!...
HEH.
OF COURSE I NOTICED IT.
OBVIOUSLY, WE'RE STILL ON THE SECOND FLOOR.

READ THIS WAY

OF COURSE!

30!

FWM
201

HEY... NOT BAD.
BUT JUST SEEING THROUGH IT ISN'T...
SNORT
...ENOUGH!!
!!

WHAP WHAP!!

HE'S SO FAST!!

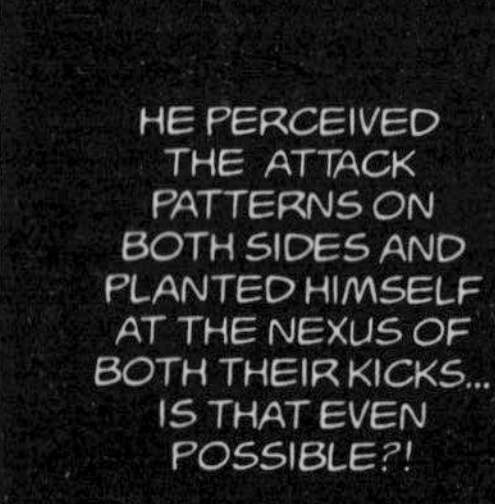
HE PERCEIVED THE ATTACK PATTERNS ON BOTH SIDES AND PLANTED HIMSELF AT THE NEXUS OF BOTH THEIR KICKS... IS THAT EVEN POSSIBLE?!

HE'S A COMPLETELY DIFFERENT PERSON FROM THE BOY WHO WAS GETTING BEATEN UP JUST A MINUTE AGO.

SLUMP
FWWU

HE BLOCKED MY KICK!
BUT THERE'S SOMETHING WEIRD ABOUT HIS CHAKRA.

WHEW
HEY...

READ THIS WAY

THAT'S NOT WHAT WE AGREED!
YOU'RE THE ONE WHO INSISTED WE SHOULD AVOID DRAWING ATTENTION TO OURSELVES.

...B... BUT...
!

BLUSH
HERE WE GO AGAIN......

GRRRR
WHAT TH...? HIS BRUISES HAVE ALREADY HEALED!

TAK TAK

UM-
!

HI. MY NAME IS ROCK LEE.
YOU'RE SAKURA, AREN'T YOU?

WOULD YOU LIKE TO GO OUT WITH ME?
GLEAM
I'LL PROTECT YOU WITH MY LIFE!

NO...
...WAY.
YOU ARE WAY OUT OF HAND!

AWWW
HEE HEE!

HEY, YOU!
STEP

WHAT'S YOUR NAME?

READ THIS WAY

IT'S ALWAYS SASUKE. SASUKE, SASUKE, SASUKE!

IT'S COMMON COURTESY TO GIVE YOUR OWN NAME FIRST.

YOU'RE A ROOKIE, AREN'T YOU? HOW OLD?
I DON'T HAVE TO TELL YOU A THING.

TAK
TAK

THIS EXAM...
...IS TURNING INTO A FREAK SHOW.

CUTE... AND COOL!
NOT A SINGLE SCRATCH!
SIGH

BONNG

HEH... SO THOSE ARE KAKASHI AND GUY'S PRECIOUS BRATS, EH? WELL, AT LEAST THEY MANAGED TO SUBMIT APPLICATIONS.
YEP.

NOW! SASUKE, NARUTO, LET'S GO!!

IT LOOKS LIKE WE CAN AMUSE OURSELVES WITH THIS YEAR'S CROP.
SNORT
A LITTLE PERK FOR BEING THE PROCTORS.

LET'S GO, LEE. WHAT ARE YOU DOING?
...

STOP PULLING.
TRA LA LA
SIGH

READ
THIS
WAY

YOU GUYS... GO ON AHEAD
THERE'S SOMETHING I WANT TO CHECK FIRST.
HEH

HEY, YOU WITH THE SCOWL... WAIT UP!!
!

!!

!!
EEP!!

WHAT IS IT?

YOU AND ME, HERE AND NOW...
WANT TO FIGHT?

NARUTO

岸本斉史

I love movies, so I go see them pretty often. And since I watch movies often, I decided to spend what little money I had to purchase a DVD player. Ho ho ho...now I can enjoy movies with incredibly high image quality and Dolby Digital sound! Or so I thought, except that the movies I wanted to watch hardly ever came out on DVD, so I couldn't watch them anyway. Recently, however, the popularity of DVDs has finally risen, and more and more DVDs are coming out!! Yes! Except...now I'm so busy drawing manga that I don't have time to watch them, even though I want to! Waah

—Masashi Kishimoto, 2000

NARUTO

NARUTO
NARUTO
VOL. 5
THE CHALLENGERS
STORY AND ART BY
MASASHI KISHIMOTO

SAKURA サクラ

Smart and studious, Sakura is the brightest of Naruto's classmates, but she's constantly distracted by her crush on Sasuke. Her goal: to win Sasuke's heart!

NARUTO ナルト

When Naruto was born, a destructive fox spirit was imprisoned inside his body. Spurned by the older villagers, he's grown into an attention-seeking troublemaker. His goal: to become the village's next *Hokage*.

SASUKE サスケ

The top student in Naruto's class, Sasuke comes from the prestigious Uchiha clan. His goal: to get revenge on a mysterious person who wronged him in the past.

KAKASHI カカシ

The elite ninja assigned to train Naruto, Sasuke and Sakura. His *Sharingan* ("Mirror-Wheel Eye") allows him to reflect and mimic enemy *ninjutsu*.

ROCK LEE ロック・リー

One of the many student ninja from foreign villages who have traveled to Konohagakure for the Junior Ninja Selection Exams. What does this creepy kid have in mind when he challenges Sasuke to a duel? Sasuke is about to find out!

THE STORY SO FAR...

Twelve years ago, a destructive nine-tailed fox spirit attacked the ninja village of Konohagakure. The *Hokage*, or village champion, defeated the fox by sealing its soul into the body of a baby boy. Now that boy, Uzumaki Naruto, has grown up to become a ninja-in-training, learning the art of *ninjutsu* with his classmates Sakura and Sasuke.

Naruto, Sasuke and Sakura have been nominated by their instructor Kakashi to take the Junior Ninja Selection Exams, which they must pass to advance to the next level of ninja training. The village is crawling with student ninja from villages near and far, who are all determined to ace the exams. On their way to turn in the applications, they observe their fellow students' advanced skill and training, and Naruto and his classmates begin to suspect that they're in way over their heads....

NARUTO

VOL. 5
THE CHALLENGERS

CONTENTS

YOU WANT TO FIGHT ME... HERE AND NOW?
BUT THAT'S...

YES!
!!
TAK
TAP

37: A TOTAL MISMATCH!!!

AMONG STICKLERS, ETIQUETTE REQUIRES ONE TO INTRODUCE ONESELF BEFORE ASKING FOR THE NAME OF ANOTHER...

MY NAME IS ROCK LEE.

...UCHIHA SASUKE.
HUH... SO YOU KNEW WHO I WAS ALL ALONG.

SHF
I'M CALLING YOU OUT!!

I WANT TO TEST THE EFFECTIVENESS OF MY TECHNIQUES...
...AGAINST THE LAST SURVIVING MEMBER OF YOUR LEGENDARY CLAN.

BESIDES...
THROB

WINK

GLARE

!

NO WAY!!
THOSE EYELASHES CREEP ME OUT!

-MWAH-
YOU'RE AN ANGEL!!
SMOOCH

...
NOT TO MENTION THE GEEKY 'DO...
PLUS THE CATER-PILLAR UNIBROW!
...
TREMBLE
TREMBLE

YIPF
!!!
...
AIEE!!
THUD

THIP
WHEW! THAT WAS TOO CLOSE...
PUFF
THROB
PUFF
THROB

SASUKE, SASUKE! IT'S ALL ABOUT SASUKE! BLEAH!
YOU KEEP YOUR WEIRD KISSES TO YOURSELF, CREEP!
I COULD HAVE DIED, DODGING THAT!!
AW... DON'T BE LIKE THAT...
SO YOU'RE CHALLENGING ME, EVEN KNOWING MY LINEAGE?
IN OTHER WORDS, YOU'RE A FOOL.
OH, YEAH!
SO, DOG-BROW... DO YOU REALLY WANT TO LEARN...
...WHAT IT MEANS TO BE AN UCHIHA?
ABSOLUTELY!
WOO
HOO!
I CAN HARDLY WAIT!
I'M GOING TOE-TO-TOE WITH THE CREAM OF THE ROOKIE CROP, FIRST TIME OUT!
NOW YOU'LL GET THE PROOF YOU REQUIRE, MASTER GUY!
HOLD IT.

JUST GIVE **ME** FIVE MINUTES...

LET ME HANDLE DOG-BROW. HE'LL BE TOAST.

ONLY UCHIHA.

I HAVE NO INTEREST IN FIGHTING YOU.

TAK TAK TAK

STORY OF MY FREAKIN' LIFE! IT'S "SASUKE, THIS!" AND "SASUKE, THAT!" TILL I COULD JUST **PUKE!**

SHHF

FWIP
!!
GURK!
THAM
SHUUM

GALE FORCE TECHNIQUE!!!
KRAK
AUGH!
THUMPITY THUMP THUMP THUMP
SPLAT

MARK MY WORDS...
NONE OF YOU WILL BEAT ME.
HE'S PRETTY TOUGH AFTER ALL. AMAZING!
I...
OOG...
...AM THE GREATEST FIGHTER AMONG ALL THE JUNIOR NINJA IN KONOHA VILLAGE!
HE STOPPED MY KICK WITH HIS ARM. NO HUMAN ALIVE CAN DO THAT. I DON'T KNOW WHAT TECHNIQUES HE'S USING... BUT I WANT TO FIND OUT!
THIS COULD BE FUN. I ACCEPT YOUR CHALLENGE.

DON'T DO IT, SASUKE!
WE HAVE LESS THAN HALF AN HOUR TO SUBMIT OUR APPLICATIONS!

12
3
6
9

!
OH!

THIS WILL ONLY TAKE FIVE MINUTES.
SASUKE!
TAK

HERE GOES!!

...I'M SORRY, MASTER GUY...I MAY HAVE TO BREAK THE BIG RULE!
I MIGHT NEED... THAT MOVE!

!!!
FWAP FWAP
KONOHA HURRICANE!!
ABOVE ME!!
SHP
!!
NO TIME TO DUCK. GOTTA BLOCK!
HOP
SHP

!!
WHUP
WHAT?!

POW

SASUKE!!!

THUD
WHAT... THE...?

I THOUGHT SASUKE BLOCKED THAT!
WHOA.

HOW'D HE GET UNDER MY GUARD?
IS THIS MARTIAL ARTS... OR MAGIC? AN ILLUSION?

THUP
AS EXPECTED, HE'S COMING BACK FOR MORE!
COME ON

UGH
FINE.
THIS MAY BE MY CHANCE TO GET IN A LITTLE PRACTICE USING... IT.

!

!
HUH?!

!!
TH - THAT LOOKS LIKE -

THE SHARINGAN MIRROR-WHEEL EYE!!

BUT WHEN COULD SASUKE HAVE...?
WHY SASUKE? AND WHY **BOTH** EYES?

SO THAT'S THE FAMOUS SHARINGAN COPYCAT EYE...

...

OH, SASUKE! HE'S THE BEST!
IF THIS IS THE SAME KIND OF GENETIC KEKKEI GENKAI SKILL THAT MASTER KAKASHI HAS, SASUKE CAN PENETRATE THE SECRETS OF DOG-BROW'S TECHNIQUES!
TAK

WHETHER IT'S A GENJUTSU ILLUSION OR A NINJUTSU FIGHTING TECHNIQUE...
THERE'S SOME KIND OF MAGIC AT WORK HERE!

AND SASUKE'S GONNA TAKE IT APART!!
HE'S GETTING STRONGER ALL THE TIME. IT MUST BE HIS UCHIHA BLOOD!
THERE'S NO WAY SOME SLIMY RUNT COULD BEAT **HIM**!

!!
HUNH?!

BUT HE USED THE SHARINGAN!

MY SHARINGAN EYE COULDN'T SEE THROUGH HIS TECHNIQUE.
BUT THAT MEANS... THOSE MOVES HE'S USING...

TAP
EXACTLY... THEY'RE NEITHER NINJUTSU NOR GENJUTSU.

VNNN

S-SASUKE!!
!!
OHH...
KAGEBUYO*... SHADOW OF THE DANCING LEAF...
WAFT

HUNH...
!

*A TAIJUTSU OR PHYSICAL ART OF THE KONOHA SCHOOL. THE USER OF THIS TECHNIQUE VISUALIZES HIS OPPONENT AS A WIND-TOSSED LEAF AND PURSUES THE LEAF BY MOVING AS ITS SHADOW.

THAT'S RIGHT. NO TRICKERY. MY MOVES ARE STRICTLY PHYSICAL.

HARD AS YOU MAY FIND IT TO ACCEPT...

I'M SURE YOUR *SHARINGAN* IS INVALUABLE AGAINST ARTS LIKE NINJUTSU AND GENJUTSU, WITH THEIR FORMALIZED RULES, SIGN-CASTING, AND CHAKRAS...
BUT PHYSICAL *TAIJUTSU* ARTS IN THEIR PURE FORM ARE A VERY DIFFERENT STORY.
... IF YOUR *SHARINGAN* EYE CAN SEE TO THE HEART OF EVERY NINJA ART WELL ENOUGH TO DUPLICATE IT, AS IT IS SAID TO, THEN YOU KNOW WHAT I SAY IS TRUE.

BUT... HOW?!

EVEN IF YOU CAN PERFECTLY PERCEIVE AND UNDERSTAND MY MOVEMENTS, YOU LACK THE SPEED AND STRENGTH TO COUNTER THEM. YOU HAVEN'T HAD THE PHYSICAL TRAINING NECESSARY TO KEEP UP WITH ME!
IT DOESN'T MATTER WHAT YOUR EYE CAN SEE IF YOUR BODY'S TOO WEAK TO ACT!

FWUP

THERE ARE TWO KINDS OF STRENGTH. THE KIND YOU'RE BORN WITH... AND THE KIND YOU ONLY GET FROM BACK-BREAKING WORK.
YOUR *SHARINGAN* IS NATURAL-BORN GENIUS. I HEAR IT RUNS IN YOUR FAMILY.
WHAT I HAVE, I GOT THROUGH BLOOD, SWEAT, AND TEARS!

IN OTHER WORDS, YOUR SUBTLE ARTS AND MY PHYSICAL PROWESS MAKE US A COMPLETE MISMATCH!
LET ME PROVE IT TO YOU.

THIS PARTICULAR MOVE OF MINE EXCEEDS YOUR GENIUS... COMPLETELY!

WHAT'S HE UP, TO?

!!
HUNH?

SLICE

HALT!
IT'S-

!!

THAT'S ENOUGH, LEE!

Number 38:
On Your Mark
YANK
THAT'S ENOUGH, LEE!

GURK!
WHAT'S... HAPPENING...?
TWIRL TWIRL
SASUKE!!!
TAK

THAM
TAP
AIEE!!
SKIIIID
YOU... YOU SAW?
SASUKE, ARE YOU ALL RIGHT?
HE'S TREMBLING... HE CAN'T EVEN DEFEND HIMSELF...
...
SASUKE GOT HIS BUTT KICKED?
THEY KNOCK ME OUT, AND I MISS ALL THE GOOD PARTS!
HE'S GETTING CHEWED OUT. AW, MAN! DON'T TELL ME THE TURTLE IS--
AHA!
AND WHAT'S THE DEAL WITH THE TURTLE?
YOU KNOW THE RULES, LEE. THAT MOVE IS STRICTLY FORBIDDEN!
P-PLEASE FORGIVE ME... I WAS ONLY...

GRRRR

EEP!

DOG-BROW'S TEACHER?!

THERE'S NO DOUBT ABOUT IT!
I... I WOULDN'T HAVE USED THE REVERSAL MOVE...I NEVER MEANT...
BUT BUT

?

TOK TOK
HEY!! HEY!
!
WHAT?

!
THAT THING OVER THERE...
THAT'S A TURTLE...
RIGHT?

OBVIOUSLY!!!
SO WHAT'S THE DEAL HERE? CAN TURTLES BECOME NINJA?
DON'T ASK STUPID QUESTIONS!!
YOU FOOL!!
...
SKKKRAPE SKRRRRAPE
DO YOU THINK I CARE ABOUT YOUR FEEBLE EXCUSES?
CONSIDER THE REPERCUSSIONS OF A SHINOBI WARRIOR-- ANY SHINOBI-- BALDLY EXPLAINING ALL HIS SECRETS!
Y-YES, SIR!
SKKKRAPE SKRRRRAPE
OHHH...
WHAT A DISGRACE, LOSING TO THAT CLOWN!
I HOPE YOU ARE PROPERLY PREPARED?
Y-YES, SIR...
WELL, THEN... HE'S ALL YOURS, MASTER GUY!
BONK

AH, THE EXUBERANCE OF YOUTH. ALL OF YOU ARE FULL OF IT.
GLARE

YAAAAAGH!!!
!!
!
TAA
DA
DAA
HE'S GOT THE BIGGEST EYEBROWS YET!
THEY'RE ALMOST... ALIVE...
THEY'RE... UBER-BROWS!
I'VE NEVER SEEN ANYTHING LIKE 'EM!
AND THAT SAME DORKY 'DO...
GRRRRR
H-HEY!! DON'T TRY TO MAKE FUN OF MASTER GUY!!
RRRRRRRR
OH, SHUT UP!
I DON'T EVEN KNOW WHAT TO MAKE OF ALL THE FREAKS WHO KEEP POPPING IN HERE!!
WHAT--
LEE!
HUNH?
OH! UH, YES, SIR...

IDIOT!!

OWW!!

BLEED

!!
HUH?!
...

YOU... YOU...
MASTER...!!

MASTER...
I... I...

THAT'S ENOUGH, LEE! NOT ONE MORE WORD.
MASTER!!
THUMP

?!
EWWW...
I GOT BEATEN... BY SOME TOUCHY-FEELY CRYBABY!

HUG
I UNDERSTAND. IT'S BECAUSE YOU'RE YOUNG!
MASTER!

DOESN'T IT GIVE YOU A WARM, FUZZY FEELING?
DON'T BE AN IDIOT! THEY'RE UP TO SOMETHING!

IT'S ALL RIGHT, LEE! MISTAKES AND YOUTH GO HAND IN HAND.
YOU ARE TOO KIND... MASTER!!
PAT

BUT I CAN'T LET YOUR ATTEMPT TO BREAK THE BIG RULE GO UNPUNISHED.
YOUR PENALTY WILL BE TO SWEAT AFTER THE *CHŪNIN* SELECTION EXAMS. ♡
I UNDER-STAND!!

FIVE HUNDRED LAPS AROUND THE PRACTICE ARENA!!
YES, SIR!!
...
WHAT A DIP...
WHAT'S THE DEAL WITH THAT TURTLE THING, ANYWAY?

READ THIS WAY

I SHOULD SAY SO! WE'RE ARCH-RIVALS!

!!! ...

HEY!
HOW'D
HE...?!
THE SCORE STANDS AT FIFTY TO FORTY-NINE.
HE...

HE'S SO FAST. HIS SPEED IS MUCH GREATER THAN MASTER KAKASHI'S!!
IS HE EVEN HUMAN?

I'M STRONGER THAN HE IS.

WHO IS THIS GUY? HE CLAIMS HE'S BETTER THAN MASTER KAKASHI...
...AND I DON'T THINK HE'S BLUFFING!

GEEZ ...
I KNOW LEE STARTED THIS FIGHT, BUT TAKE PITY ON HIS OLD TEACHER. FOR THE SAKE OF MY OWN SELF-RESPECT, FORGIVE HIM.
GOTTA SAVE FACE... IT'S JUST SO HANDSOME!

AS YOU CAN SEE, MASTER GUY IS TOTALLY AMAZING!!!

CHUK

YOU AND LEE SHOULD HEAD UP TO THE CLASSROOM NOW.
!!!
...
POF

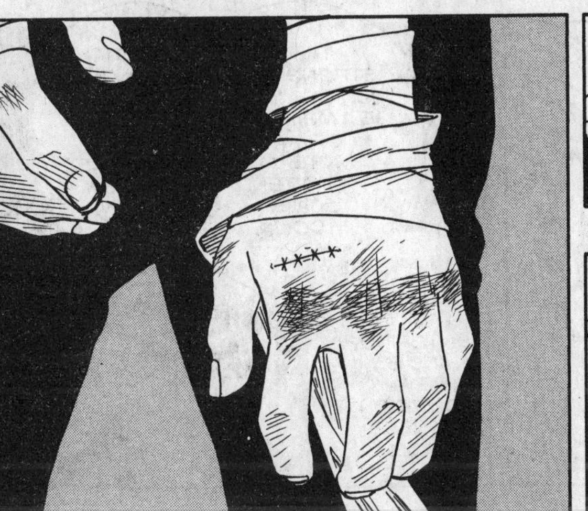

!

FLAP

!!
HE'S...

FLUP
FLUP

TAK
BEST OF LUCK, LEE!
LATER!!
YES, SIR!

BY THE WAY, SASUKE...
...I WAS BLOWING SMOKE BEFORE.
I'M REALLY HERE TO PROVE MY OWN STRENGTH IN COMBAT.
YANK

AND I DON'T THINK YOU'RE THE STRONGEST KONOHA GENIN.
THE STRONGEST JUNIOR NINJA IS A MEMBER OF MY OWN TEAM... ...AND I INTEND TO TAKE HIM DOWN.
THAT'S WHY I'M ENTERING. AND BY THE WAY... YOU'RE ON MY LIST, TOO.

OFF TO APPLY FOR THE EXAM. BE READY FOR IT, OKAY?
HOP
...

KRUNCH

SASUKE...
WHAT WAS THAT CRAP?!

... SHUT UP...
NARUTO!!
MAYBE YOUR HOT-SNOT, FAMOUS UCHIHA CLAN ISN'T THAT GREAT AFTER ALL, HUH?

DESPITE THE TOTAL BUTT-KICKING YOU GOT THIS TIME, RIGHT?
SHUT UP, NARUTO!

NEXT TIME, HE'S DEAD MEAT.

YOU SAW HIS HANDS, RIGHT?

GRRRRR

OLD DOGGY BROWS PROBABLY GETS SOME KIND OF SUPER-DUPER EXTRA-SPECIAL TRAINING, DAY AFTER DAY!

EVEN MORE THAN YOU GOT.

YOU'RE TOAST, PAL!

INTERESTING...

...

YEP!
WELL, YEAH!

THINGS ARE STARTING TO GET INTERESTING. THIS *CHŪNIN* SELECTION EXAM IS BRINGING THINGS TO A BOIL!

NARUTO? SAKURA? LET'S GO!

YEAH!!

GLAD YOU MADE IT AFTER ALL, SAKURA.
THIS WAY YOU ALL QUALIFY TO APPLY FOR THE *CHŪNIN* SELECTION EXAM.
!
...WHAT DO YOU MEAN?
THE WAY THE TEST IS SET UP, IT CAN ONLY BE TAKEN BY THREE-PERSON CELLS.
BUT... MASTER KAKASHI, YOU SAID IT WAS UP TO EACH OF US TO DECIDE WHETHER OR NOT TO APPLY. WERE YOU LYING?

I SAID WHAT I HAD TO TO KEEP YOUR PARTNERS FROM PRESSURING YOU INTO COMING ALONG.
EVEN IF YOU HAD NO INTEREST IN APPLYING, ONE WORD FROM SASUKE...
...AND YOU'D HAVE COME ALONG AND GONE THROUGH THE MOTIONS, THOUGH YOUR HEART WOULDN'T HAVE BEEN IN IT.

WHAT WOULD HAVE HAPPENED IF SASUKE AND NARUTO HAD SHOWN UP WITHOUT ME?
I'D HAVE WASHED THEM OUT RIGHT HERE. NONE OF YOU WOULD HAVE GOTTEN PAST THIS POINT WITHOUT BOTH OF THE OTHERS.

BUT YOU'RE ALL HERE BECAUSE YOU WANT TO BE. AND I'M VERY, VERY PROUD OF YOU.
NOW GET IN THERE!

CREAK
LOOK OUT EVERYBODY, 'CAUSE HERE WE COME!!

WINK

39: THE CHALLENGERS!!

TAK

TAK

TAK

!!!

39: The Challengers!!

SO MANY PEOPLE.
ARE THEY ALL HERE TO APPLY?
HUGGG
SASUKE! WHERE'VE YOU BEEN, CUTIE? ♡
!!
THEY LOOK... INCREDIBLE...
ULP!
I COULD HARDLY WAIT! IT'S SO EXCITING, SEEING YOU AGAIN AFTER ALL THIS TIME!
INO, YOU PIG!!! GET YOUR HOOVES OFF SASUKE!
HELLO TO YOU, TOO, SAKURA.
STILL HOPING THE BIG, MUTANT FOREHEAD LOOK IS GOING TO COME INTO FASHION, HUH? HOW SWEET. ♡

WHAT DID YOU SAY?!
BLEAH!
WHY DON'T YOU THREE SAVE YOURSELVES THE EMBARRASSMENT OF FLUNKING THIS TEST? GO DIE, OKAY?

WELL, IF IT ISN'T THE THREE STOOGES!
TAK
STOP CALLING US THAT!
MUNCH
UNCH

WHAT A PAIN IN THE BUTT.
ASUMA CELL NUMBER 10
NARA SHIKAMARU
A LAZY, UNMOTIVATED, GOOD-FOR-NOTHING, FULL OF NOTHING BUT COMPLAINTS.
WHINING FOOL.

MUNCH
UNCH
ASUMA CELL NUMBER 10
AKIMICHI CHOJI
A LITTLE PORKER WHO'S ALWAYS STUFFING HIS FACE.
FAT FOOL.

GONNA MAKE SASUKE MINE! ♡ BLEAH!
ASUMA CELL NUMBER 10
YAMANAKA INO
SAKURA'S RIVAL AND ARCH-NEMESIS, AND ANOTHER WOULD-BE SASUKE GROUPIE.
FOOL FOR SASUKE.

HEY! THERE YOU ARE!
SHINOBI
OOH!

UH... HI...
LOOKS LIKE THE GANG'S ALL HERE.

INCLUDING YOU... UNFORTUNATELY!

SO... I GUESS ALL THREE OF THIS YEAR'S NEWBIE TRIOS DECIDED TO APPLY, HUNH?
TAK
TAK
I WONDER HOW FAR WE'LL ALL GET.
WHAT DO YOU THINK... ...SASUKE?

TRYING TO PSYCH US BY ACTING COOL, KIBA?

WHO'S ACTING? THE WAY **WE'VE** TRAINED, NO WAY CAN YOU BEAT US.
HEE HEE HEE!
OH, SHUT UP!! YOU GUYS WON'T EVEN BEAT ME, MUCH LESS SASUKE!

GRRRRR
HUNH?

THAT DOG WOULD PROBABLY BE GREAT WITH SOME HOT SAUCE......
MUNCH
MUNCH

KIBA DIDN'T MEAN THAT THE WAY IT SOUNDED...
I-I'M SORRY, NARUTO...
UMM
UMM
UH

KURENAI CELL NUMBER 8
INUZUKA KIBA AND AKAMARU
A WORSE WILDMAN THAN ME! HE MAKES ME SICK, DRAGGING THAT STUPID MUTT EVERYWHERE AND TRYING TO THROW HIS WEIGHT AROUND!

KURENAI CELL NUMBER 8
HYUGA HINATA
A WORLD-CLASS FREAK WHO WON'T EVEN LOOK ME IN THE EYE. A SHY LITTLE BRUNETTE.

WOULD YOU GUYS...
...DO US ALL A FAVOR AND JUST SHUT UP?
!!

KURENAI CELL NUMBER 8
ABURAME SHINO
I DON'T KNOW THIS GUY FROM ADAM. NO READING ON HIM WHATSOEVER.

TAK
YOU THREE GANGS OF WOULD-BE HOTSHOTS ARE ALL GENIN, RIGHT? KIDS BARELY OUT OF THE LOCAL NINJA ACADEMY?
ALL WET-BEHIND-THE-EARS AND RUNNY-NOSED!
THIS ISN'T A SCHOOL FIELD TRIP, YOU KNOW.
WHO THE HECK DO YOU THINK YOU ARE?
NAME'S KABUTO. SO WHAT?
WHY?
YOU KIDS NEED TO OPEN YOUR EYES.
GRRRR

READ THIS WAY

WATCH OUT FOR THE GROUP BEHIND YOU. THEY'RE AMAGAKURE-- THOSE-WHO-HIDE-IN-THE-RAIN-- AND THEY'VE GOT VERY SHORT FUSES.
EVERYONE'S ON EDGE, WAITING TO TAKE THE EXAM. I WANTED TO GIVE YOU A HEADS-UP BEFORE SOMEONE SNAPS AND BEATS THE CRAP OUT OF YOU.
OH.

BUT IT'S PROBABLY UNAVOIDABLE. LIKE ALL ROOKIES, YOU THINK YOU ALREADY KNOW EVERYTHING.
I REMEMBER WHAT IT WAS LIKE.

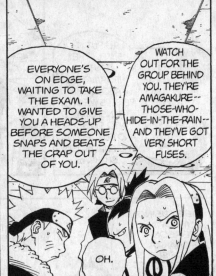

KABUTO?
YEAH?
ARE YOU SAYING THIS IS THE SECOND TIME YOU'VE APPLIED?

NOT SECOND...
SEVENTH.
TWICE A YEAR FOR... HM, GOING ON FOUR YEARS NOW.

WOW-- THEN YOU'VE GOT A LOT OF EXPERIENCE WITH WHAT WE CAN EXPECT!
I GUESS SO.
ALL RIGHT! KABUTO, BUDDY... YOU ARE THE MAN!! ♡

CUTE. OKAY... THE LEAST I CAN DO IS GIVE YOU SWEET LITTLE BABIES SOME VITAL INTELLIGENCE ON WHAT YOU'RE IN FOR...
...WITH THESE *SHINOBI* SKILL CARDS.
FLIP

SHINOBI SKILL CARDS?

TO PUT IT SIMPLY, THEY CONTAIN INFORMATION ABOUT THE SKILLS WE USE, TRANSFORMED INTO SYMBOLS AND BURNED INTO THE CARDS USING CHAKRAS.
TAP

SHF
IT TOOK ME FOUR YEARS TO COLLECT ALL THE INTELLIGENCE NEEDED FOR THIS EXAM.
IN ALL, THERE ARE ALMOST 200 CARDS.

FLIP
FLIP
FWUP
THEY LOOK BLANK, DON'T THEY? THE ONLY WAY YOU CAN READ THE DATA ON THE CARDS...

WHAT'S HE DOING?
...IS BY USING MY OWN PERSONAL CHAKRA. EACH SET IS LINKED TO ITS POSSESSOR. FOR EXAMPLE, CARDS LIKE THIS ONE...
ONNNNG

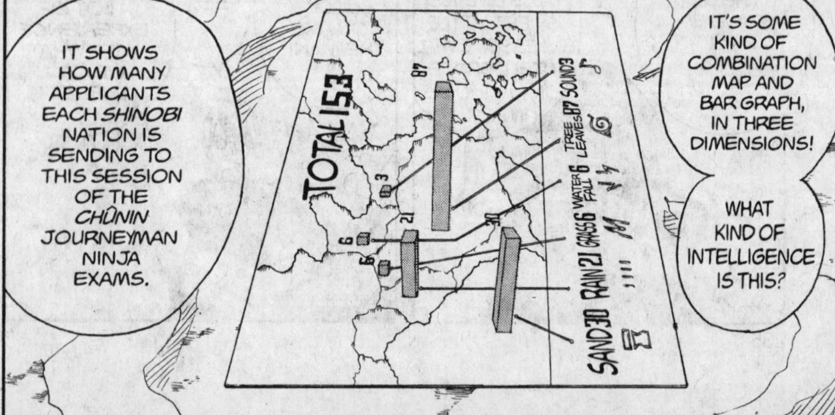
IT'S SOME KIND OF COMBINATION MAP AND BAR GRAPH, IN THREE DIMENSIONS!
WHAT KIND OF INTELLIGENCE IS THIS?
IT SHOWS HOW MANY APPLICANTS EACH *SHINOBI* NATION IS SENDING TO THIS SESSION OF THE *CHŪNIN* JOURNEYMAN NINJA EXAMS.
TOTAL 153
87
3
21
6
6
30
SAND 30
RAIN 21
GRASS 6
WATER FALL 6
TREE LEAVES 87
SOUND 3

DO YOU ALSO HAVE DOSSIER CARDS? CARDS FOR EACH INDIVIDUAL APPLICANT?
HA HA ... WHY? SOMEONE HERE YOU HAVE A PARTICULAR INTEREST IN?

I'LL ADMIT THESE ARE FAR FROM COMPLETE, BUT I'VE BURNED A SET OF DOSSIER CARDS FOR THE CURRENT POOL OF APPLICANTS...

...INCLUDING YOUR TEAM. IF YOU SHARE ANY DATA YOU HAVE ON THIS PERSON WHO INTERESTS YOU, I'LL BE HAPPY TO LOOK HIM UP AND LET YOU KNOW WHAT I HAVE SO FAR.
FLIP

GAARA, FROM SUNAGAKURE--HIDE-IN-SAND--AND ROCK LEE, FROM KONOHA.
YOU KNOW THEIR NAMES? NO SWEAT, THEN!

FLIP

I DON'T HAVE A CLUE WHAT THIS GUY'S TALKING ABOUT... BUT I'LL PLAY ALONG.

LET ME SEE THEM.

FIRST UP IS ROCK LEE.

HE'S A YEAR OLDER THAN YOU THREE. MISSIONS TO DATE: 20 D-RANKED, 11 C-RANKED. HIS TEAM'S MENTOR IS MIGHT GUY...

AND HIS *TAIJUTSU* PHYSICAL SKILLS HAVE GROWN EXPONENTIALLY THIS PAST YEAR. HE HAS NO OTHER TALENTS WORTH MENTIONING.

HE WAS CONSIDERED A STANDOUT AMONG LAST YEAR'S *GENIN*... BUT HE DIDN'T APPLY FOR THE *CHÛNIN* EXAM.

HE'S A FRST-TIMER, LIKE YOU THREE. HIS TEAMMATES ARE NAMED HYUGA NEJI AND TENTEN.

NEXT IS GAARA OF THE SAND... DESERT COUNTRY...

EIGHT C-RANKED MISSIONS... ONE B. WOW! NOT MANY ROOKIE SHINOBI GET B-RANKED ASSIGNMENTS!

SINCE HE'S FROM WAY OUT IN THE DESERT, I HAVE LESS ON HIM... BUT IT'S INTERESTING. HE'S COME BACK FROM EVERY MISSION COMPLETELY UNSCATHED.

WITHOUT A SCRATCH...

...

READ THIS WAY

KONOHA, SUNA, AME, KUSA, TAKI, OTO... THIS YEAR, EVERY HIDDEN VILLAGE HAS SENT OUTSTANDING JUNIOR-LEVEL GENIN HERE TO COMPETE.
I DON'T KNOW MUCH ABOUT OTO, THE VILLAGE HIDDEN IN SOUND. IT'S PART OF A NEW, SMALL NATION, SO INTELLIGENCE ON IT IS LACKING.
EVERY OTHER COMPETING VILLAGE IS WELL-RESPECTED, HOME TO SOME FORMIDABLY POWERFUL SHINOBI...

WHAT YOU'RE TRYING TO TELL US IS... EVERYONE HERE...
ANYBODY BESIDES ME SUDDENLY FEELING KIND OF OUTCLASSED?

OH, YEAH. THEY'RE ALL LIKE LEE AND GAARA...
ELITE, HAND-PICKED SHINOBI, THE BEST YOUNG NINJA IN THE WORLD.

THEY HAVE TO BE! THE TEST IS PITILESS!

301

IT'S A HARSH AND UNFORGIVING TEST, KAKASHI!
YOU'RE RUSHING THEM INTO IT!

IRUKA WAS RIGHT!
MY KIDS ARE THE BEST, BUT I STILL GAVE THEM A YEAR TO MATURE BEFORE LETTING THEM APPLY.
GIVE YOUR CELL TIME TO BUILD SOME STRENGTH.
HEH...

WHAT MY KIDS LACK IN EXPERIENCE, THEY MORE THAN MAKE UP IN SURPRISES, GUY.

YOUR CELL WILL EAT THEIR DUST.

BAH!

ENOUGH OF THIS.

FOR OUR NEXT ORDER OF BUSINESS, I'LL CONSIDER RECOMMENDATIONS FOR GENIN CANDIDATES WHO HAVE PASSED THEIR FIRST YEAR.

HAH!
OVER ONE HURDLE...

EVEN SO....
THOSE THREE ARE UTTERLY FEARLESS...
... BUT EVEN THEY MUST BE A LITTLE UNEASY, WONDERING WHAT COMES NEXT.
301

SHIVER
SHIVER

LOOKS LIKE EVEN OUR TEAM'S OVERCONFIDENT BUTTHEAD HAS THE SHAKES.
SHIVER

AND WHO CAN BLAME HIM? WE'RE ALL GENIN HERE...
BUT WE THREE ARE THE YOUNGEST... ABSOLUTE BEGINNERS!

STILL, IT'S NOT LIKE NARUTO. MAYBE IF I GIVE HIM A LITTLE PEP TALK...
IT'S ALL RIGHT, NARUTO. NOTHING TO WORRY ABOUT.

!

MY NAME IS UZUMAKI NARUTO!!
AND NONE OF YOU ARE GONNA BEAT ME!!!!
ONNNNG
!!

YOU GOT THAT?
...

WHAT'S HIS PROBLEM?!
TYPICAL. TOO STUPID TO KNOW HE'S GOT PROBLEMS.

YEAH!
THAT FELT GREAT!

OH, PLEASE!

...
DIDN'T WE MEET HIM EARLIER?

KID'S GOT SOME LIFE IN HIM.
MAYBE YOU WENT TOO EASY ON HIM, LEE.

SO... ACCORDING TO THIS DOSSIER, OUR TOWN IS AN UNKNOWN LITTLE VILLAGE IN A BACKWATER COUNTRY.
MORTIFYING, ISN'T IT?

WANT TO HAVE SOME FUN WITH THEM?

SOUNDS GOOD!

THAT TWIT, TREATING US LIKE SOME KIND OF AFTERTHOUGHT. LET'S GIVE HIM A LITTLE DATA FOR HIS DOSSIER. HIS UNDERSTANDING OF THE VILLAGE HIDDEN IN SOUND IS... UNSOUND.

WE'LL SEE WHERE THE INTELLIGENCE IS LACKING...

40: The First Test

"AND NONE OF YOU ARE GONNA BEAT ME!" THE NERVE OF THAT KID!
LITTLE SHOW-OFF!
THAT IDIOT TURNED A ROOM FULL OF STRANGERS INTO A ROOM FULL OF ENEMIES WITH JUST ONE SENTENCE.

WHAT ARE YOU BLATHERING ABOUT?!
I'M TELLING THE TRUTH!!

GRRRRR

PAY NO ATTENTION TO MY FRIEND...
HE'S... YOU KNOW... A SPECIAL-ED NINJA...
ACK

WHAT WERE YOU THINKING?!
SHALL WE?

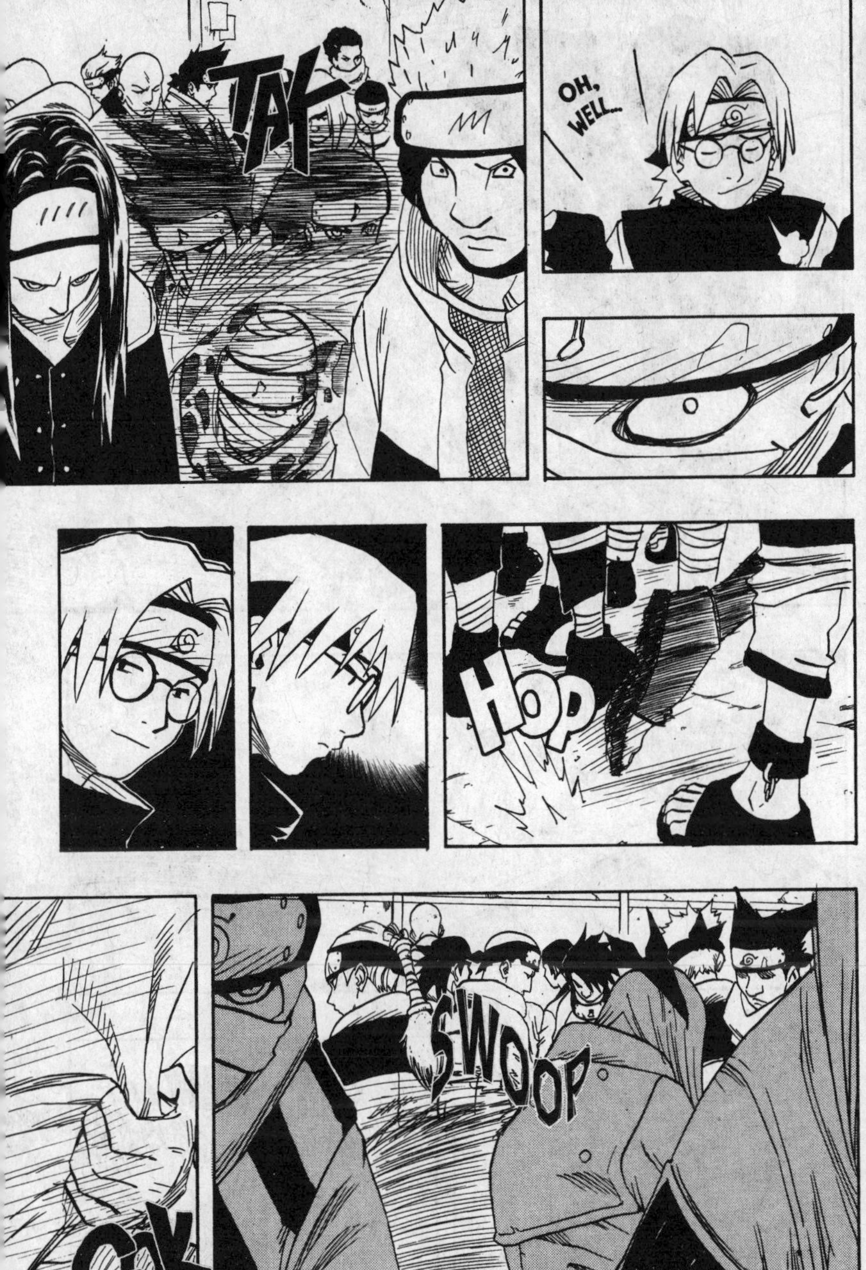
OH, WELL...
TAK
HOP
SWOOP
GOK

CRAB

CRAB

TAP

!!
FWN
POO
SHING
SHING
VWN VWN VWN
!!!
SKF
THOK
THOK
SHF SHF SHF SHF
FWIP
POOF

!!
THEY'RE FROM SOUND...
!!

HE DODGED IT!

SO QUICKLY I BARELY SAW HIM MOVE.

!
KRAK

PLINK
PLINK

!

I SEE. THIS KIND OF AT-TACK...
...IS...
HMMM...
PLUCK
PLINK

WHAT'S GOING ON? HE DODGED THE BLOW, BUT SOMETHING BROKE HIS GLASSES!
HIS NOSE PROBABLY GOT GRAZED...
SERVES HIM RIGHT FOR ACTING ALL SUPERIOR.

?!
SHUDDER

BLORCH

SPLATTER

AW, MAN! HE'S HURLING!

KABUTO?

NOTE: ABUMI'S SHIRT SAYS "DEATH."

HMPH.

死
死
死

KABUTO!! HEY, BRO!

ARE YOU ALL RIGHT?

...YEAH... I'M FINE...

YOU DON'T LOOK FINE.

YOU'RE A PUSHOVER, AREN'T YOU? PRETTY SAD FOR SOMEONE WHO'S BEEN AN APPLICANT FOR FOUR YEARS NOW.

SORRY TO HAVE KEPT YOU WAITING.
MY NAME IS MORINO IBIKI. I'M THE PROCTOR AND CHIEF EXAMINER FOR THE FIRST PART OF THE EXAM.

ULP!

YOU... THE KIDS FROM THE SOUND VILLAGE! YOU CAN'T CARRY ON ANY WAY YOU PLEASE WHEN THE EXAM'S ABOUT TO START!
...OR DO YOU WANT TO BE DISQUALIFIED?

SORRY, SIR.... IT'S OUR FIRST EXAM, AND WE GOT A LITTLE CARRIED AWAY.

IS THAT SO?
THEN IT'S HIGH TIME SOMEONE LAID DOWN A FEW GROUND RULES.
FROM THIS POINT FORWARD, THERE WILL BE NO MORE FIGHTING WITHOUT THE EXPRESS PERMISSION OF THE EXAMINING OFFICER...
AND EVEN IF THAT PERMISSION IS GRANTED, ANYTHING THAT ENDANGERS ANOTHER APPLICANT'S LIFE IS STRICTLY FORBIDDEN.

ANY OF YOU LITTLE PIGLETS WHO BREAK THAT RULE ARE OUT. DISQUALIFIED. NO SECOND CHANCES.
GOT THAT?

...

SO THIS IS A TEST FOR LITTLE GIRLY MEN?

SNEER

AS YOU WISH. THE FIRST PART OF THE SELECTION EXAM IS ABOUT TO COMMENCE.
TURN IN YOUR WRITTEN APPLICATIONS, TAKE ONE OF THESE SEATING ASSIGNMENT CARDS...

... AND REPORT DIRECTLY TO THE SEAT INDICATED.
1
FLIP
WHEN EVERYONE'S SEATED, WE'LL PASS OUT THE WRITTEN PART OF THE TEST.

HUNH?
?
?

A- A PAPER TEST?!

THIS MUST BE NARUTO'S WORST NIGHTMARE. HE LOOKS ABSOLUTELY CRUSHED!
AW, MAN-- WE'RE SPREAD OUT ALL OVER THE ROOM.
NOW WHAT DO I DO?
NARUTO...
53
53

OH! I DIDN'T EVEN SEE YOU, HINATA.
THIS CHICK'S A REGULAR INVISIBLE GIRL!
L-LET'S DO OUR BEST!

NOW LISTEN UP. PAPERS FACE DOWN UNTIL I GIVE THE SIGNAL.

TAP TAP
THERE ARE A FEW BIG RULES THAT PERTAIN TO THIS FIRST TEST.
I'LL WRITE THEM ON THE BLACKBOARD AND EXPLAIN THEM ALL, BUT I'M NOT TAKING QUESTIONS, SO LISTEN CAREFULLY. I WILL SAY THIS ONLY ONCE.

RULES?
AND NO QUESTIONS?! WHY NOT?

RULE NUMBER ONE! EACH ONE OF YOU STARTS OUT HERE WITH TEN POINTS.
THE TEST HAS TEN QUESTIONS, EACH WORTH ONE POINT.
FOR EACH QUESTION YOU GET WRONG, WE SUBTRACT A POINT FROM YOU.
SKRITCH
SKRITCH

GET ALL TEN RIGHT, AND YOU RETAIN THE TEN POINTS YOU HAVE.

TOTAL POINTS

EXAMPLE 1.
PERFECT SCORE
TOTAL POINTS
REMAIN AT 10

EXAMPLE 2.
3 ANSWERS WRONG
TOTAL POINTS
ARE REDUCED TO 7 POINTS

BUT IF, FOR EXAMPLE, YOU ANSWER THREE QUESTIONS INCORRECTLY, WE TAKE YOUR TEN POINTS...

...SUBTRACT ONE POINT FOR EVERY WRONG ANSWER... AND YOUR TOTAL DROPS DOWN TO SEVEN.

IN OTHER WORDS, IF I GET ALL TEN QUESTIONS WRONG, I'LL END UP WITH NO POINTS AT ALL!

RULE NUMBER 2... THIS WRITTEN TEST IS STILL A TEAM EVENT.
PASSING OR FAILING WILL BE DETERMINED BY THE SUM OF THE POINTS HELD BY ALL THREE MEMBERS OF EACH CELL.

BAM
THE OBJECT IS FOR EACH TEAM TO HAVE AS FEW DEDUCTIONS AS POSSIBLE FROM ITS JOINT THIRTY-POINT TOTAL.
CRAP
W-WAIT A SECOND!
THE WHOLE CONCEPT OF THE STARTING POINTS AND THE DEDUCTIONS IS HARD ENOUGH TO FOLLOW... BUT WHAT IS THIS "TEAM TOTAL" YOU'RE TALKING ABOUT?
HOP

DID YOU NOT HEAR THE PART ABOUT "NO QUESTIONS"? WE HAVE OUR REASONS.
SHUT UP AND LISTEN. YOU MIGHT LEARN SOMETHING.

THIS NEXT BIT IS CRUCIAL.
WHAT REASONS...?

RULE NUMBER 3: IF, DURING THE COURSE OF THE EXAM, A CANDIDATE DOES ANYTHING OUT OF THE ORDINARY...

...IN OTHER WORDS, ANYTHING THAT LEADS THE PROCTORS TO DETERMINE THAT HE OR SHE HAS CHEATED...

...WE SUBTRACT TWO POINTS FROM EACH MEMBER OF THE CHEATER'S TEAM.

OH!
EXACTLY! IN ALL PROBABILITY, SOME OF YOU WILL RUN THROUGH YOUR ENTIRE ALLOWANCE OF POINTS DURING THE TEST. IF SO, YOU'LL BE FAILED AND ASKED TO LEAVE.
I GET IT...
THERE ARE MORE WAYS TO LOSE A POINT THAN JUST MISSING A QUESTION.
I'LL BE LOOKING OVER YOUR SHOULDERS WHEN YOU LEAST EXPECT IT.
YIIPE!!
IF YOU LET THE PROCTORS CATCH YOU CHEATING, YOU'LL BRING YOURSELF AND YOUR FRIENDS DOWN!
IF YOU ASPIRE TO BECOME CHÛNIN...
...IF YOU WANT TO BE THE BEST SHINOBI YOU CAN BE...
... THEN YOU'D BETTER START ACTING LIKE YOU ALREADY ARE!
YES

GET A HOLD OF YOURSELF, SAKURA. IT'S TOO BAD ABOUT NARUTO, BUT SASUKE AND I SHOULD BE ABLE TO RETAIN ENOUGH POINTS FOR ALL THREE OF US...
...EVEN IF NARUTO GETS EVERY SINGLE ANSWER WRONG!

ONE MORE THING...
IF ANY INDIVIDUAL LOSES ALL TEN OF HIS OR HER POINTS, THAT PERSON'S ENTIRE CELL, REGARDLESS OF HOW THE OTHER TWO MEMBERS DO...

...WILL BE DISQUALIFIED!!

!!
WHAT?!

WHAT?!

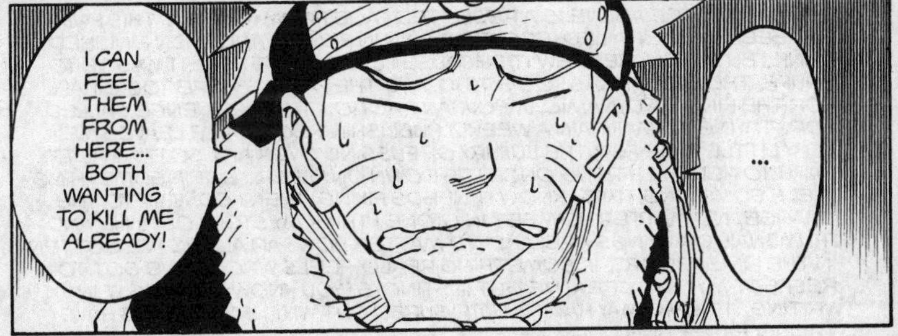
...
I CAN FEEL THEM FROM HERE... BOTH WANTING TO KILL ME ALREADY!

KISHIMOTO MASASHI'S "I ONLY SHOW YOU THESE THINGS SO YOU'LL UNDERSTAND HOW MUCH I LOVE MANGA" REJECTS CORNER...

THE MANGA PAGE ABOVE IS A REJECTED PAGE FROM NARUTO. THIS PAGE HAD BEEN THUMBNAILED, BROKEN DOWN IN PENCIL, AND THEN FINISHED IN INK... BUT I STILL REDREW IT, BECAUSE I JUST DIDN'T FEEL IT WAS UP TO SNUFF. THE LAYOUT WAS TOO STATIC, AND THE PANELS WERE TOO SMALL FOR THE KIND OF DYNAMIC, IMPORTANT ACTION THIS SEQUENCE CALLED FOR. TRYING TO MAINTAIN A WEEKLY PUBLISHING SCHEDULE LEAVES ME VERY LITTLE TIME FOR THE LUXURY OF FUSSING OVER ART, SO IT'S PRETTY RARE TO REDO ANYTHING ONCE IT'S DOWN ON PAPER... BUT IF SOMETHING FEELS SO WRONG THAT I KNOW IT NEEDS FIXING, THEN I COMMIT TO THE CHANGE, NO MATTER HOW SET IN STONE I THINK MY STORY OUTLINE AND THUMBNAIL DRAWINGS ARE, AND NO MATTER HOW FAR ALONG I'VE GOTTEN IN THE FINISHED ART. IF SOMETHING REALLY FEELS WRONG, I'VE GOT TO RESPECT MY OWN CREATIVE GUT INSTINCTS. YOU KNOW... SEEING IT IN WRITING... I THINK I MAY HAVE JUST FIGURED OUT WHY I SOMETIMES HAVE TROUBLE MEETING DEADLINES!

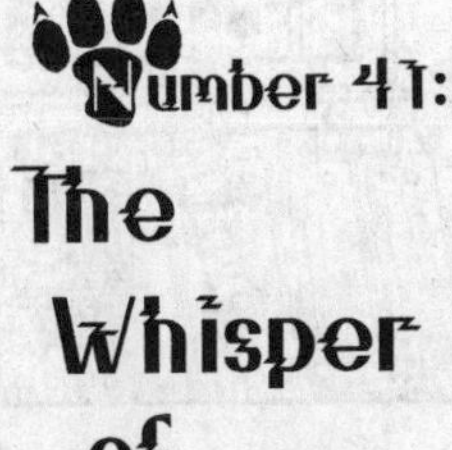

THE *CHÛNIN* JOURNEYMAN NINJA SELECTION EXAM
RULES FOR PART ONE

(1) EACH APPLICANT BEGINS WITH A PERFECT SCORE OF TEN POINTS. THERE ARE TEN QUESTIONS WORTH ONE POINT APIECE. A POINT IS SUBTRACTED FOR EVERY INCORRECT ANSWER. THE GRADING SYSTEM IS ENTIRELY BASED ON A PRINCIPLE OF PENALIZATION.

(2) THE EXAM IS A TEAM EVENT. WHAT MATTERS IS HOW CLOSE EACH THREE-NINJA CELL CAN COME TO RETAINING ITS INITIAL THIRTY POINTS.

(3) ANYONE CAUGHT ATTEMPTING TO CHEAT OR AIDING AND ABETTING A CHEATER WILL LOSE TWO POINTS FOR EACH OFFENSE.

(4) ANYONE WHO HAS NO POINTS LEFT AT THE TEST'S END--WHETHER DUE TO BEING CAUGHT CHEATING OR TO AN INABILITY TO ANSWER ANY OF THE QUESTIONS CORRECTLY--WILL AUTOMATICALLY FAIL; IF A SINGLE INDIVIDUAL FAILS, THE REMAINING TWO MEMBERS OF THAT PERSON'S CELL WILL BE FAILED AS WELL.

...STARTING...
JLP!

YOU HAVE ONE HOUR...

...NOW!

...TRY TO HANG ON TO AT LEAST **ONE** OF YOUR POINTS!!

...SAY IT ISN'T SO...
THIS COULD BE A NO-WIN SITUATION...
PLEASE, NARUTO!...

SCRATCH
SCRATCH

HEH...

HEH HEH HEH... THIS IS FUNNY...

HEE HEE HEE

HERE I AM AGAIN... FACING THE WORST KIND OF ENEMY! TEACHERS DIDN'T CALL ME THE ALL-TIME DUNCE FOR NOTHING!

I EARNED THAT NAME ON THE FIELD OF BATTLE!

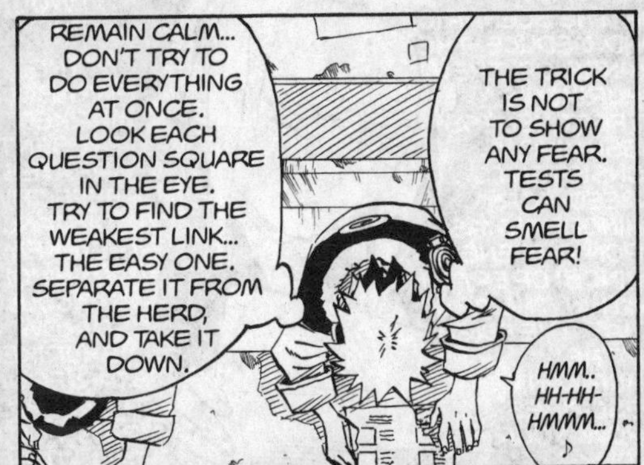
THE TRICK IS NOT TO SHOW ANY FEAR. TESTS CAN SMELL FEAR!
REMAIN CALM... DON'T TRY TO DO EVERYTHING AT ONCE. LOOK EACH QUESTION SQUARE IN THE EYE. TRY TO FIND THE WEAKEST LINK... THE EASY ONE. SEPARATE IT FROM THE HERD, AND TAKE IT DOWN.
HMM.. HH-HH-HMMM... ♪

...
SHIVER SHIVER

THIS IS SO NOT GOOD!
NARUTO IS AN IDIOT... I JUST HOPE HE DOESN'T PANIC.
WHOA. FIRST UP IS CRYPTO-GRAPHY.
THEY WANT US TO WORK OUR BUTTS OFF!
CHŪNIN JOURNEYMAN NINJA SELECTION EXAM PART ONE
QUESTION NO. 1
DECODE THE FOLLOWING CIPHER AND SUMMARIZE ITS MEANING.
...

...I WONDER HOW NARUTO'S DOING...
NEXT!

...BUT I'VE GOT TO CON-CEN-TRATE ON MY OWN WORK!
I'VE GOT TO HANG ONTO ALL MY POINTS, TO MAKE UP FOR HIM...

UM... NUMBER TWO...
"THE PARABOLA MARKED B REPRESENTS THE GREATEST EFFECTIVE DISTANCE THE ENEMY SHINOBI, A, COULD THROW A SHURIKEN STAR FROM THE TOP OF A 23.3-FOOT-TALL TREE...
"CALCULATE THE SPECIFIC FEATURES OF THE SCENARIO AND DEDUCE THE RANGE OF THE SHURIKEN'S EFFECTIVENESS, ASSUMING A CONSISTENT SPEED FOR SHINOBI A'S ASSAULT UPON ANY ENEMY SHINOBI OPERATING WITHIN THE ARC THAT THE FLIGHT OF THE SHURIKEN DESCRIBES. SHOW YOUR WORK."

THIS... THIS IS... TO SOLVE THIS, YOU NEED TO HYPOTHESIZE UNDER VERY UNCERTAIN CONDITIONS... AND THEN APPLY THE LAWS OF KINETICS TO WHATEVER YOU COME UP WITH!

THERE'S NO WAY NARUTO COULD SOLVE SOMETHING LIKE THIS!!
OF COURSE, NEITHER CAN MOST OF THE PEOPLE HERE. IT'S A KILLER...
'COURSE, I CAN ANSWER IT.

HMF.

WH-O-O-SH

HEH...
HEH.

WELL, WELL...
I DON'T KNOW HOW TO ANSWER A SINGLE ONE OF THESE QUESTIONS.
SIGH

QUESTION NUMBER 10
THIS QUESTION WILL NOT BE PROVIDED UNTIL FORTY-FIVE MINUTES INTO THE EXAM.
AT THAT TIME, PLEASE ANSWER THE PROCTOR'S QUESTION TO THE BEST OF YOUR ABILITY.
AND WHAT'S THE DEAL WITH NUMBER TEN?

G-R-O-A-N
AW...
MAN, HOW AM I GONNA GET OUT OF THIS?!

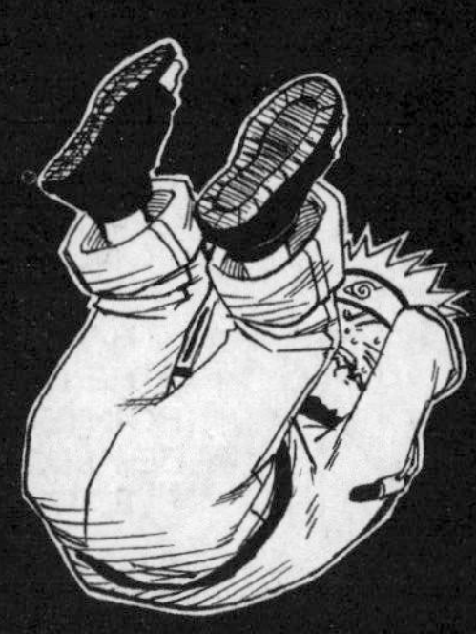
WHAT DO I DO?
WHAT DO I DO?
WHAT DO I DO?
WHAT DO I DO?
WHAT DO I DO?
WHAT DO I DO?
WHAT DO I DO?
WHAT DO I DO?
WHAT DO I DO?
WHAT DO I DO?

ARGH!

GRRRR...
I'VE GOT TO BE SLY... SNEAKY...
...

THEY'RE WATCHING US.
LIKE CATS WATCH MICE. LIKE THEY EXPECT US TO CHEAT. THOSE RATS!

RULE NUMBER 2...

...MAKES IT PRETTY CLEAR THAT WE'RE COMPETING AGAINST EACH OTHER. OBVIOUSLY, ONLY THE TEAMS THAT KEEP THE MOST POINTS WILL BE ALLOWED TO PASS.
I JUST WISH I KNEW WHERE THE CUT-OFF LIES- HOW MANY OF THE TOP TEAMS CAN PASS...

NOT THAT KNOWING WOULD CHANGE ANYTHING...
BUT THE UNCERTAINTY IS DRIVING ME NUTS.

YOU KNOW... THE ONE THING I KEEP WONDERING...
SCRAPE
!

...IS HOW MANY OF THE TOP-RANKING TEAMS THEY INTEND TO PASS.
...

HEE-HEE-HEE-HEE-HEE!
!
!

KNOWING THAT NOW ISN'T GOING TO HELP YOU, IS IT?
UNLESS YOU'RE HOPING TO FAIL.

I-I'M SORRY...
I THOUGHT SO!
SKFF

IF ONLY ABOUT TEN OF THE FIFTY-ONE TEAMS HERE CAN PASS...
... ALL THREE OF US HAVE TO RETAIN AS MANY POINTS AS POSSIBLE.

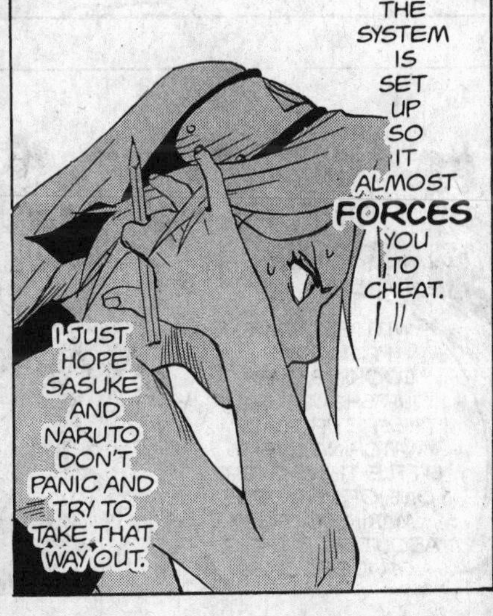
THE SYSTEM IS SET UP SO IT ALMOST FORCES YOU TO CHEAT.
I JUST HOPE SASUKE AND NARUTO DON'T PANIC AND TRY TO TAKE THAT WAY OUT.

...BUT THEY WOULDN'T. THEY COULDN'T. NOT EVEN NARUTO IS THAT STUPID...
...IS HE?
REMAIN CALM...
ABOVE ALL, PROCEED WITH CAUTION.

MY ONLY HOPE IS TO CHEAT SO WELL THEY DON'T CATCH ME!!!

...

WHAP-WHAP-WHAP
NO WAY! NO WAY! DON'T EVEN THINK ABOUT IT!
DANGER! DANGER! DO NOT GO THERE!

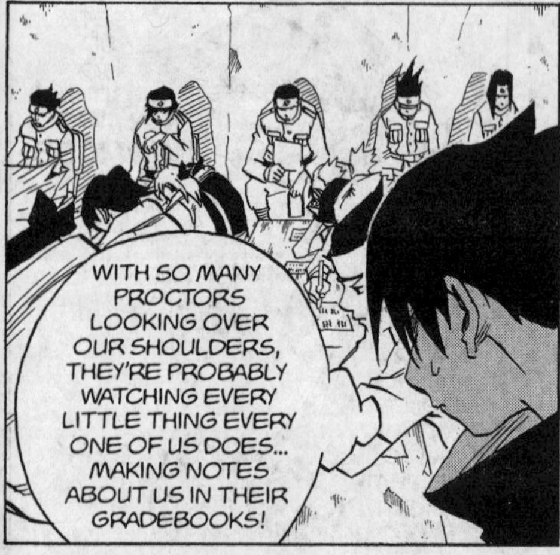

WITH SO MANY PROCTORS LOOKING OVER OUR SHOULDERS, THEY'RE PROBABLY WATCHING EVERY LITTLE THING EVERY ONE OF US DOES... MAKING NOTES ABOUT US IN THEIR GRADEBOOKS!

SCRATCH
SCRATCH

!
THE AXE HAS FALLEN SOMEWHERE!

IF YOU LET THE PROCTORS CATCH YOU CHEATING, YOU'LL BRING YOURSELF AND YOUR FRIENDS DOWN!

IF YOU ASPIRE TO BECOME CHÛNIN... ...IF YOU WANT TO BE THE BEST SHINOBI YOU CAN BE... ... THEN YOU'D BETTER START ACTING LIKE YOU ALREADY ARE!
...

!!
HOLD IT!!

...
NOW I GET IT!!
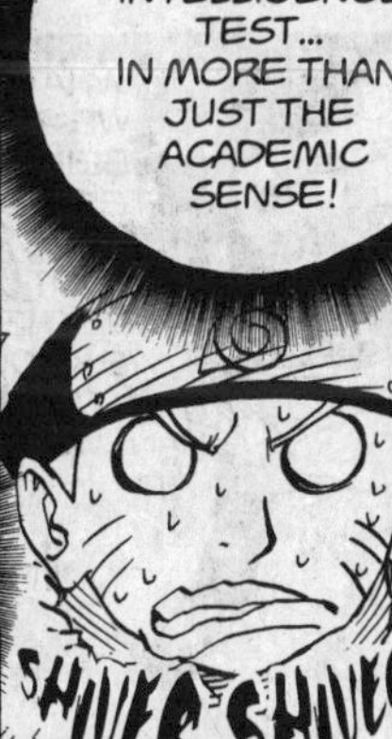
UNBELIEVABLE... THIS IS AN "INTELLIGENCE" TEST... IN MORE THAN JUST THE ACADEMIC SENSE!
SHIVER SHIVER

WAKE UP, NARUTO!

YOU'RE HISTORY IF YOU DON'T FIGURE IT OUT!
THEY'RE ALSO TESTING...

...OUR INFORMATION-GATHERING SKILLS!
THEY WANT US TO CHEAT... LIKE SHINOBI! WITHOUT GETTING CAUGHT!

SHINOBI MUST LEARN TO UNCOVER THE SECRETS WITHIN SECRETS. THE PROCTORS WANT US TO CHEAT...
...REALLY WELL! THE WAY THE BEST SHINOBI WOULD, IF THEY NEEDED THIS KIND OF INFORMATION IN A REAL-WORLD MISSION!

LOOK AT HOW THEY SET UP THE "PERFECT SCORE, MINUS PENALTIES" SCENARIO! WITH TWO POINTS DEDUCTED EVERY TIME YOU GET CAUGHT CHEATING...
...THE REAL MESSAGE IS THAT YOU CAN BE CAUGHT FOUR TIMES BEFORE YOU FACE DISQUALIFICATION!

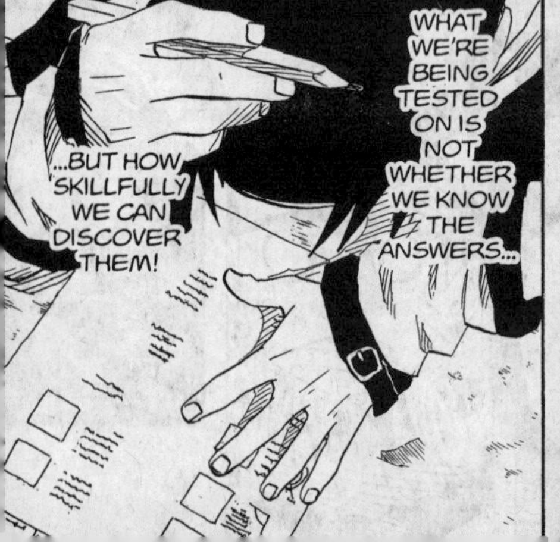
WHAT WE'RE BEING TESTED ON IS NOT WHETHER WE KNOW THE ANSWERS...
...BUT HOW SKILLFULLY WE CAN DISCOVER THEM!

COME ON, NARUTO!
ANY MINUTE NOW, EVERYONE WHO'S FIGURED IT OUT WILL START GOING FOR IT!

GRRR

STOP GLARING AT ME.
I GET IT, ALREADY.

YAWN

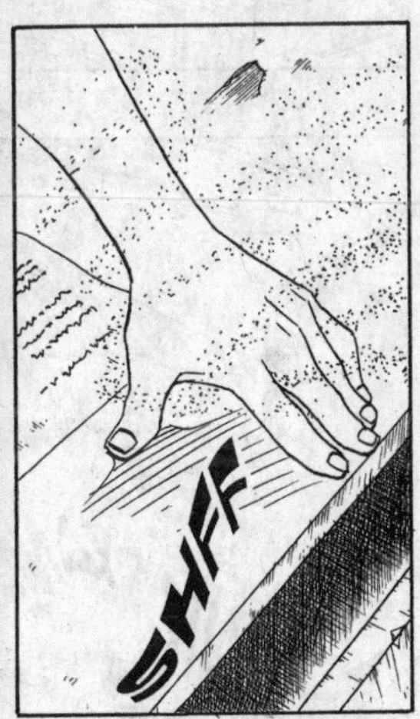
SHFF

GAARA'S STARTED, TOO, HUH?
DON'T FAIL ME, SCARE-CROW...

PEEEK
PEEEK

WOOF! WOOF! WOOF!
WOO-HOO! GOOD BOY, AKAMARU! NEXT IS QUESTION NUMBER 4...

SCRATCH SCRATCH

NNNNNNN

EXCELLENT! TELL ME MORE!

BZZZZZZ
NUMBER EIGHT, HUNH?

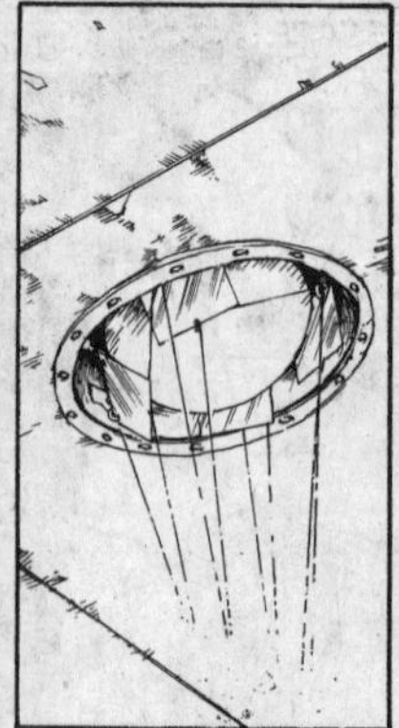

YANK
YANK

YANK YANK
LEE, IF YOU CAN SEE IT, ADJUST YOUR HEADBAND...

TUG

SCRATCH SCRATCH

SCRATCH
SCRATCH
SCRATCH

FROM THE RHYTHM, THE WRITING ORDER, AND NUMBER OF STROKES THAT GO INTO THE WORDS...

SCRATCH SCRATCH
...GOT IT...

BYAKUGAN! THE ALL-SEEING EYE!
SHF
SHF
THAT'S THE ONE. I'M GOING TO MIMIC HIS EVERY...
...MOVE!

USING THE SHARINGAN COPY EYE!!
ON
NG

TICK
TOCK

RATS!!
IF I DON'T CHEAT, I'M DEAD ANYWAY!

AAAARGH!
I'M ALMOST OUT OF TIME!

!!
WHOOSH

!!
AAH!!
TH
OK

READ
THIS
WAY

THAT WAS CLOSE...
I WAS ABOUT TO TURN AROUND.

WH-WHAT WAS THAT FOR?

THAT'S FIVE STRIKES...
...AND YOU'RE OUT!

N...
NO WAY...

TAKE YOUR TEAMMATES WITH YOU. OUT OF THIS CLASSROOM.
NOW.

READ THIS WAY

DANG!
YOU'RE DONE HERE. MOVE IT!
TRUDGE TRUDGE

YIPE! THAT WAS TOO CLOSE. NO WAY AM I GONNA RISK CHEATING... NOT ALONE!
N-NARUTO...

!
YOU CAN LOOK AT MY PAPER, IF YOU WANT TO...

HUNH?

Number 42:

To Each His Own

NARUTO... PLEASE...
LOOK AT MY ANSWERS.

WH- WHAT'S HINATA TALKING ABOUT?
WHY WOULD SHE HELP ME?

...

!!
OH... NO! NO WAY!

!
IT MUST BE SOME KIND OF TRICK!
GRRRR

BLUSH
...

BUT THAT WOULD BE SUCH A DIRTY TRICK... HINATA'S NOT THAT KIND OF GIRL...
UNLESS KIBA AND THE OTHERS PUT HER UP TO IT... FORCED HER.

LEVEL WITH ME!
WHAT'S IN IT FOR YOU IF YOU HELP ME?!

OHHHHH

IT'S... IT'S JUST...

...

FIDGET
FIDGET

I... ...YOU...

ULP!

I DON'T WANT YOU... TO HAVE TO LEAVE SO SOON, NARUTO.

...
?

W-WELL, YOU KNOW... THERE ARE ONLY NINE OF US NEWBIES, AND WE DON'T KNOW WHAT WE'RE FACING...
FLUTTER FLUTTER
...THE ODDS WILL BE BETTER FOR ALL OF US... IF WE STICK TOGETHER... AT LEAST FOR NOW...

OH... OKAY. HEH... I GUESS THAT MAKES SENSE...
SORRY FOR DOUBTING YOU.
HAH!

BOY!
THIS IS MY LUCKY DAY.
GOOD THING HINATA WAS NEXT TO ME!

HMM-HH-HHMM...♪
PEEK

!!
SCRATCH
SCRATCH
EH?

SCRATCH
SCRATCH

...

HINATA...
DON'T YOU GET IT?

HUH?

A WORLD-CLASS NINJA LIKE ME JUST ISN'T THE KIND OF GUY WHO CHEATS!

I-I'M SORRY I BOTHERED YOU...
HEY, NO PROBLEM.

GREAT. SHE BELIEVED ME. NOW I'VE GOT MY HONOR...
AND I'M SCREWED!
...TRYING TO BE A BIG SHOT.

TICK
TICK
11 12 1 2 3 4 5 6 7 8 9 10

THE TEST'S BEEN GOING FOR HALF AN HOUR... ONLY ANOTHER HALF LEFT!
TICK
TICK

SCRATCH
SCRATCH
SCRATCH
SCRATCH
SCRATCH

AT THIS POINT...
...THAT LAST QUESTION IS MY ONLY HOPE.

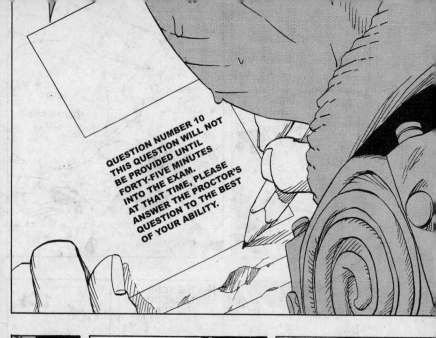

QUESTION NUMBER 10
THIS QUESTION WILL NOT BE PROVIDED UNTIL FORTY-FIVE MINUTES INTO THE EXAM. AT THAT TIME, PLEASE ANSWER THE PROCTOR'S QUESTION TO THE BEST OF YOUR ABILITY.

THAT'S IT! I'VE ANSWERED THEM ALL!
THERE'S NOTHING LEFT FOR ME TO DO BUT WAIT FOR THE TENTH QUESTION.

I'VE BEEN WRITING NON-STOP.
I WAS GOING TO TRY TO MIMIC TWO OR THREE OTHER STUDENTS TO BE ON THE SAFE SIDE...
SCRATCH
SCRATCH

BUT I HIT THE TARGET DEAD-CENTER ON MY FIRST TRY.
SCRATCH
SCRATCH

IT LOOKS LIKE SAKURA HAS FINALLY STOPPED WRITING. ♡
TIME TO MAKE MY MOVE! ♡

SAKURA... YOUR BROAD BROW AND BIG BRAIN HAVE EARNED MY RESPECT...

...SO YOU OUGHT TO FEEL HONORED... ♡

...THAT YOU'RE GOING TO BE THE TARGET OF MY SIGNATURE TECHNIQUE! ♡
WELL THEN, HERE IT COMES... ♡

SLUMP

INO'S ASLEEP.

SHE MUST BE USING THAT TECHNIQUE OF HERS...

NO ONE CAN WITHSTAND HER WHEN SHE STARTS THAT ASTRAL-PROJECTION STUFF!

ZZZ

!!

!

ZZAP

OH-HH...

HEH HEH HEH...

SORRY, SAKURA... NOT.

SAKURA...

YOU'RE A DEAR, LETTING ME POSSESS YOU LIKE THIS... AND SEE ALL OF YOUR ANSWERS! ♡

YES!
GOT IT!
HAVE TO MEMORIZE THIS QUICKLY, BEFORE SOMEONE CATCHES ME. ♡
NEXT I'LL POSSESS SHIKAMARU AND CHOJI, AND WRITE THESE ANSWERS ON THEIR PAPERS! CLEVER LITTLE ME! ♡

ON YOUR FEET, NUMBER 102.
YOU FAIL.

NO WAY!!

YOU TOO, NUMBER 23.

YOU'RE OUT!

TICK

TOCK

DANG...

D...

SLAM

THAT'S THIRTEEN CELLS THEY'VE FLUNKED OUT SO FAR!

TICK

NUMBER 43 AND NUMBER 27... START WALKING.

YOU ALL FAIL!

TOCK

POW
AAGH!!
!!
YOU FEEL THIS? WELL, I AM AS SKILLED AS I AM POWERFUL!
GULP!
!!!
OW...
LISTEN UP AND LISTEN GOOD. WE PROCTORS ARE THE ELITE. EVEN IN A GROUP AS SKILLED AS THE ONE GATHERED HERE TODAY, WE ARE FAR AND AWAY THE BEST. WE MISS NOTHING!
YOU GOT THAT, KIDS?

READ THIS WAY

HMMF...
THAT BRAT IS UP TO SOMETHING!

WHATEVER IT IS, HE'S DOING IT WITHOUT TURNING A HAIR... PERFECTLY CALM IN THE EYE OF THIS HURRICANE.
SHF

FOR A ROOKIE, HE'S AMAZING.

SKITTER
ITTER

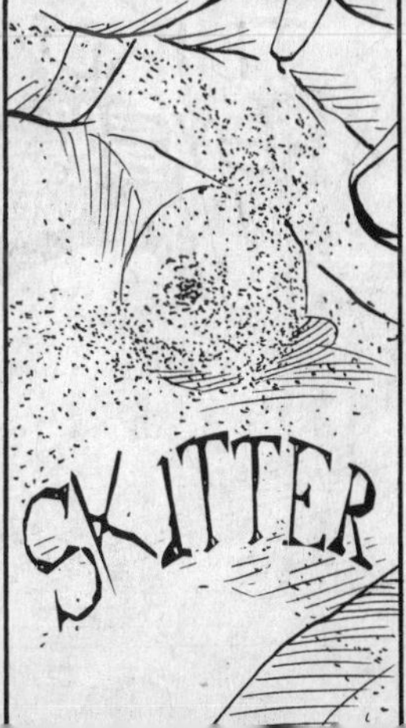
SKITTER

POK

MY OPTIC NERVE IS RECONNECTED ...
...OPENING MY THIRD EYE!!

SQUISH

SKUFF

PUFF

FLOAT

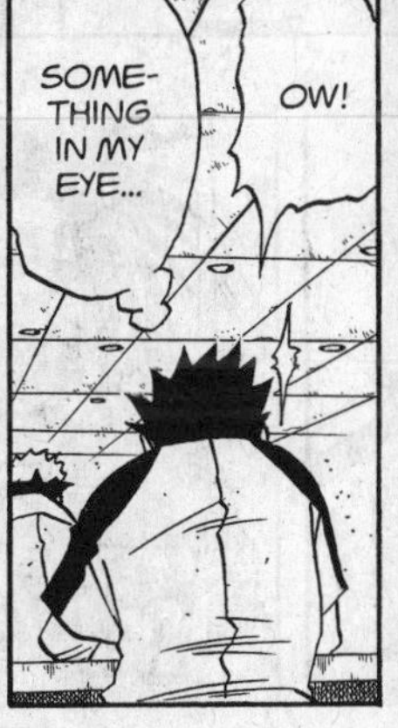
OW!
SOME-THING IN MY EYE...

BLAST IT...!
FLOAT

CHŪNIN JOURNEYMAN
NINJA SELECTION
EXAMINATION

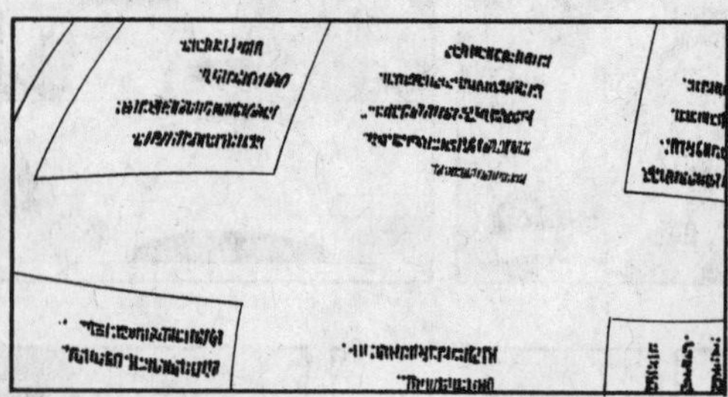

OWW...!

SCRATCH
SCRATCH

EXCUSE ME.
WHAT IS IT?

I'VE GOT TO GO TO THE BATH-ROOM...

OF COURSE. ONE OF THE PROCTORS WILL ACCOMPANY YOU.
WHY NOT?

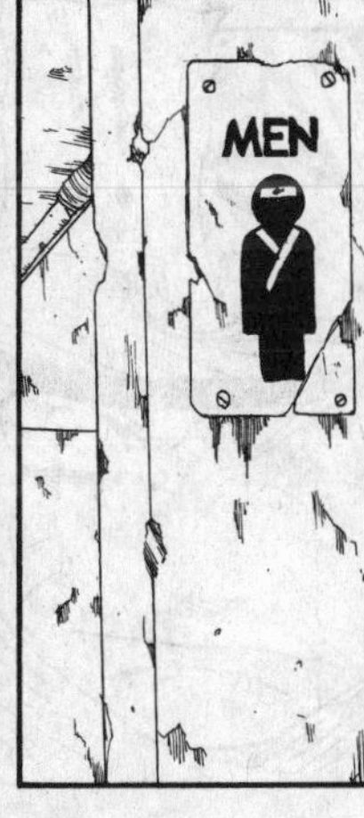
MEN

THEY THINK THEY'RE SO SLICK!

AND THEY NEVER EVEN NOTICED THAT THERE'S BEEN ONE EXTRA PROCTOR THIS WHOLE TIME!
PRETTY SAD!
CRUMBLE

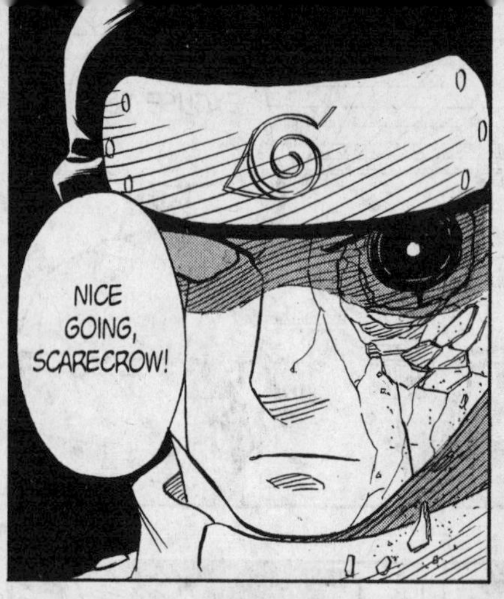
NICE GOING, SCARECROW!

SIGH...
SHIVER
...NOW THEN, GIVE ME ALL THE ANSWERS IN ORDER, STARTING WITH NUMBER ONE. HEH HEH HEH...
SHIVER

NOW THAT WE'VE WEEDED OUT THE WORST OF THE SLACKERS...
LET'S MOVE ON TO THE MOST IMPORTANT QUESTION.
FORTY-FIVE MINUTES HAVE PASSED. THE TIME HAS COME.

CORRECT?
GET READY FOR THE TENTH QUESTION!

!!
HERE IT COMES!!

ALL RIGHT! HERE IT COMES.
GET READY FOR THE TENTH QUESTION.

Number 43: The Tenth Question

RRRRR
...!!
I'M RISKING IT ALL ON ONE ROLL OF THE DICE.

JUST ONE MORE MOUNTAIN TO CLIMB!
MR. BIG SHOT... HA!

YOU BETTER HURRY BACK, KANKURO!
I WAS SUPPOSED TO GET YOUR FIRST NINE ANSWERS BEFORE THEY GAVE US THE TENTH QUESTION.

AND BEFORE WE GET TO THE QUESTION ITSELF...
...I'M ADDING ONE MORE NEW RULE.

!!?

VVVVN

HEH...
LOOKS LIKE YOU'RE IN LUCK.
?!

THE TIME YOU'VE SPENT PLAYING WITH DOLLS HASN'T BEEN COMPLETELY WASTED.
DOLLS... DOES HE KNOW ABOUT SCARECROW?

DON'T WORRY ABOUT IT. SIT DOWN.

SNEAK

LET ME EXPLAIN.
FWP

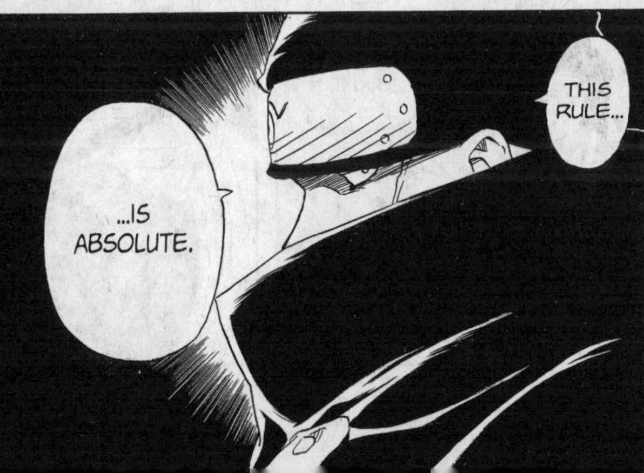
THIS RULE...
...IS ABSOLUTE.

WOW...
JINSEI IROIRO
* JINSEI IROIRO: "THERE ARE MANY DESTINIES."
WITH OUR SUBORDINATES TIED UP IN EXAMS, WE'VE GOT TIME ON OUR HANDS.
IT'S NOT LIKE WE CAN GO ON TRAINING MISSIONS WITHOUT THEM.
SIGH
DON'T WORRY. WE'LL BE BUSY AGAIN BEFORE YOU KNOW IT.
WHY?
WORD IS, THIS YEAR'S FIRST CHIEF EXAMINATION OFFICER IS MORINO IBIKI.
...
THAT SADIST? WHY DID IT HAVE TO BE IBIKI?!
!
SADIST?
WILL THEY EVEN MAKE IT PAST THE FIRST EXAM?
KURENAI, YOU'RE STILL A NEWBIE TO THE JÔNIN ELITE, SO YOU HAVE NO WAY OF KNOWING.

READ
THIS
WAY

...
WHY? WHAT'S HE LIKE?

HE'S A PRO. A PRO'S PRO...
A PRO?
AT WHAT ?
SIZZLE

TORTURE AND INTERROGATION!
SIGH

....!
HUNH?

KONOHA BLACK OPS
TORTURE AND INTERROGATION CORPS UNIT LEADER
JÔNIN COMMANDER
MORINO IBIKI!

IN THE EXAM THAT'S PRESENTLY UNDERWAY... WHILE THERE MAY BE NO PHYSICAL TORTURE...
...THERE'S NO DOUBT THAT THE APPLICANTS ARE BEING SUBJECTED TO THE PSYCHOLOGICAL PRESSURES THAT MAKE HIM INFAMOUS AS AN INTERROGATOR.

AN ABSOLUTE RULE...?!
ULP!

FIRST... YOU MUST CHOOSE...
...WHETHER TO ACCEPT OR REJECT THIS TENTH QUESTION!

ACCEPT OR REJECT...?

CH-CHOOSE?
WHAT HAPPENS IF SOMEONE DOESN'T ACCEPT THE QUESTION?!

IF YOU REJECT THE QUESTION AND DON'T EVEN TRY TO ANSWER IT, YOU'LL LOSE ALL YOUR POINTS IMMEDIATELY...
...AND FAIL!
AND BOTH OF YOUR TEAMMATES WILL FAIL RIGHT ALONG WITH YOU.
SAY WHAT?!
THEN WHY WOULD ANYONE CHOOSE TO REJECT IT?
BECAUSE...
...OF THE OTHER RULE.
!
OH, COME ON. WHAT MORE CAN HE ADD?!
IF YOU TRY TO ANSWER THE QUESTION...
...AND YOU GET IT WRONG...
...YOU WILL NEVER BE PERMITTED TO APPLY FOR THE JOURNEYMAN NINJA EXAMS AGAIN. NOT EVER.
ONNNNNG
!!

YOU CAN'T BE SERIOUS. THAT'S RIDICULOUS!!!
THERE ARE NINJA HERE WHO'VE SAT FOR THE *CHÛNIN* EXAMS MORE THAN ONCE ALREADY!! WE KNOW THERE ARE!
WUFF
HEH HEH...
HEH HEH HEH HEH.
!!
...

JUST YOUR ROTTEN LUCK. I WASN'T MAKING THE RULES IN PAST YEARS.
I AM NOW.

I'VE BEEN UP FRONT WITH YOU. YOU CAN TAKE A FAILING GRADE NOW, AND TRY AGAIN LATER.
HUH?
ANYONE WHO HAS DOUBTS WOULD BE SMART TO REJECT THE TENTH QUESTION RIGHT NOW.
COME BACK AND REAPPLY NEXT YEAR, AND THE YEAR AFTER THAT.

TALK ABOUT A NO-WIN SITUATION!

IF EVEN ONE MEMBER OF A CELL REJECTS THE QUESTION, THEN ALL THREE TEAM MEMBERS FAIL FOR THE YEAR.

IF ANYONE ACCEPTS THE QUESTION AND CAN'T ANSWER IT...

HE'LL BE STUCK AT THE JUNIOR LEVEL FOR THE REST OF HIS LIFE!

HEADS YOU WIN, TAILS WE LOSE!!
NO SANE PERSON COULD MAKE SUCH A CHOICE!!

READY?
THEN LET'S BEGIN.

THOSE WHO CHOOSE NOT TO ACCEPT SHOULD RAISE THEIR HANDS.
ONCE THEIR NUMBER HAS BEEN CONFIRMED, THEY WILL LEAVE THE ROOM.

HUUUUUUSH

WHAT KIND OF STUPID QUESTION COULD IT BE?!

IF I GET IT WRONG, I'LL BE A JUNIOR-GRADE ROOKIE FOR LIFE... NOT ACCEPTABLE!!
BUT IF I JUST REJECT THE QUESTION...

...SASUKE AND SAKURA BOTH HAVE TO SUFFER FOR MY LACK OF GUTS.

READ THIS WAY

I DON'T INTEND TO RAISE MY HAND.
I'M SURE I CAN ANSWER THE QUESTION, WHATEVER IT MAY BE!

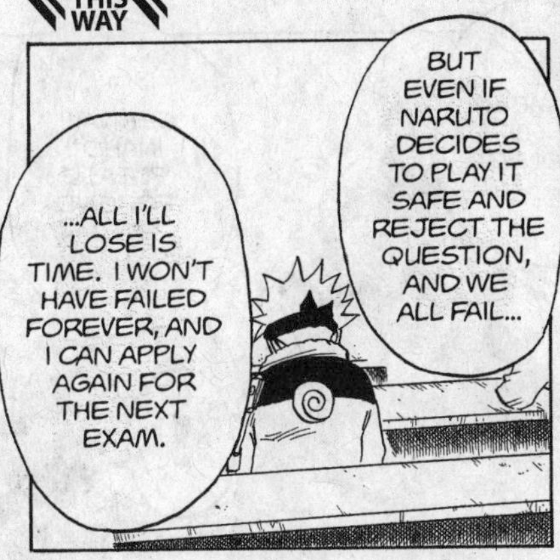
BUT EVEN IF NARUTO DECIDES TO PLAY IT SAFE AND REJECT THE QUESTION, AND WE ALL FAIL...
...ALL I'LL LOSE IS TIME. I WON'T HAVE FAILED FOREVER, AND I CAN APPLY AGAIN FOR THE NEXT EXAM.

BUT...

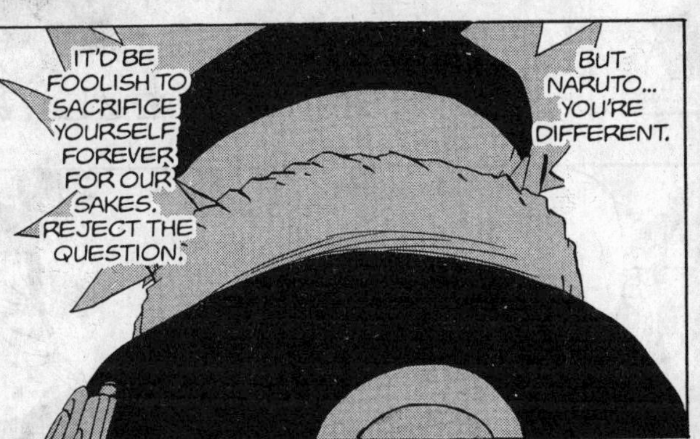
BUT NARUTO... YOU'RE DIFFERENT.
IT'D BE FOOLISH TO SACRIFICE YOURSELF FOREVER FOR OUR SAKES. REJECT THE QUESTION.

SHF

I-I...
...
!
KLATTER

I QUIT! I'M REJECTING THE QUESTION!

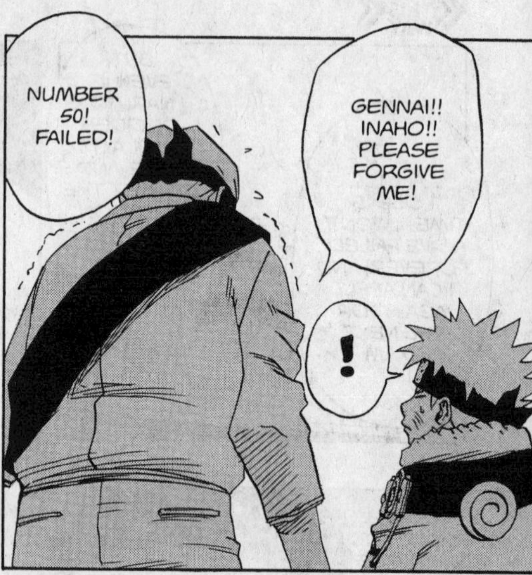
GENNAI!! INAHO!! PLEASE FORGIVE ME!
!
NUMBER 50! FAILED!

NUMBER 130! NUMBER 111! YOU FAIL RIGHT ALONG WITH HIM.

CLATTER
CLATTER

CURSES...
...

ME TOO...
I QUIT, TOO!!
I-I'M SORRY, GUYS!!
TAK
ME TOO...

M-ME TOO!!

...NARUTO...
WHY DON'T YOU RAISE YOUR HAND?

...
THAT IDIOT!

I... I DID IT! I DID IT! I'M A NINJA!
NINJA! NINJA! NINJA!

IT'S UZUMAKI NARUTO.
I AM THE CREAM OF THE ELITE. IN FACT, ONE DAY I'M GONNA BE THE NEXT LORD HOKAGE! SO REMEMBER MY NAME.

WELL, YOU'RE OLD AND STUPID!
I AM DOING ALL THE RIGHT THINGS, AND I'M DOING THEM FAST.

...I'LL BE A BETTER SHINOBI THAN LORD HOKAGE!!
...AND THEN ALL THE VILLAGERS WILL HAVE TO ACKNOWLEDGE MY EXISTENCE AT LAST!!

HE'S ALWAYS GOING ON ABOUT "LORD HOKAGE" THIS AND "HOKAGE" THAT...
...LIKE A BROKEN RECORD!

I'M SORRY, NARUTO...
YOUR DREAM MAY BE CRAZY...

...BUT I DON'T WANT IT TAKEN AWAY FROM YOU FOREVER.

KRUNCH

!
HUNH?
FREEZE

THAT IBIKI...
...UNDERSTANDS THE HUMAN HEART COMPLETELY. IT'S WHAT MAKES HIM SO TERRIBLE.

HE USES HIS INSIGHTS MERCILESSLY TO MANIPULATE HIS FOES... BRINGING THEIR HUMAN WEAKNESSES TO THE SURFACE...

...AND USING THOSE WEAKNESSES TO MAKE THEM CRACK!

TRICKERY IS NO DEFENSE AGAINST HIS SKILLS AS AN INTERROGATOR.
SHIVER
SHIVER

N...
NARUTO...!!

!!
!!

SHUDDER
SHUDDER

NEVER UNDERESTIMATE ME!!!
SLAM
I DON'T QUIT, AND I WON'T RUN!!

I'LL ACCEPT YOUR STUPID QUESTION!!

EVEN IF I RISK ENDING UP A ROOKIE FOR THE REST OF MY LIFE...

...I'LL STILL BECOME LORD HOKAGE, EVEN IF I CAN ONLY MAKE IT BY PURE STUBBORNNESS. I DON'T CARE!!

I'M NOT AFRAID OF YOU!!

SNORT
...

HE... NEVER EVEN GAVE US A THOUGHT.
BUT HE CERTAINLY DOES HAVE GUTS.

GOOD THING...
BECAUSE AN IDIOT LIKE HIM NEEDS THEM!

I'LL ASK YOU ONE LAST TIME.
THIS IS A DECISION THAT COULD AFFECT THE REST OF YOUR LIFE.
QUIT NOW, WHILE YOU STILL HAVE THE CHANCE.

I NEVER GO BACK ON MY WORD.
THAT'S... MY SHINOBI WAY!

SEVENTY-EIGHT OF THEM ARE STILL HERE.
HMMM... AN ENTERTAINING KID, AND INTERESTING. HE DISPELLED EVERYONE ELSE'S DOUBTS ALONG WITH HIS OWN.
MORE THAN I EXPECTED, BUT...

NOD
NOD

...THERE'S NO POINT IN DRAGGING IT OUT. THANKS TO HIM...
...NO ONE ELSE WILL QUIT.

GULP!

GOOD CALL.
SO, EVERYONE WHO IS STILL HERE...

...YOU'VE JUST PASSED THE FIRST EXAM!!!

!!
HUNH?!!!

A FRIEND OF MINE DREW THIS PICTURE OF NARUTO FOR ME.

Number 44:
The Talents We Test For

SO...ALL SEVENTY-EIGHT OF YOU WHO ARE STILL HERE...
...YOU'VE JUST PASSED THE FIRST EXAM.
!!!
...
WHAT DO YOU MEAN, "PASSED"?
WHEN DID THAT HAPPEN?
WHAT ABOUT THE TENTH QUESTION?!

READ THIS WAY

THERE IS NO TENTH QUESTION...
...BEYOND THE WHOLE "ACCEPT OR REJECT" THING.
gr
in

HUNH?!!
!

HEY! THEN WHY DID WE HAVE TO SUFFER THROUGH THE OTHER NINE QUESTIONS?!
THAT WAS A TOTAL WASTE OF OUR TIME!

THERE WAS NO WASTE.
THOSE QUESTIONS HAD A PURPOSE, WHICH THEY'VE ALREADY SERVED.

!
SUCH AS?

OUR GOAL WAS TO TEST YOUR SKILLS...
...AT SPYING!

?
HE SEEMS LIKE A COMPLETELY DIFFERENT PERSON.
...OUR SKILLS AT SPYING?

REMEMBER THE RULES AT THE BEGINNING?
YOU PASS OR FAIL AS PART OF A THREE-MAN CELL.
WITH THAT RULE, I PRESSURED YOU WITH THE FEAR THAT ANYTHING YOU DID WRONG...
...WOULD BRING YOUR TEAMMATES DOWN WITH YOU.
OH, I GET IT!

YOU KNOW, I KINDA FIGURED THAT WAS IT.
YOU ARE SO FULL OF IT!

YEP!

TEE HEE...

HOWEVER... THE QUESTIONS ARE BEYOND THE LEVEL THAT JUNIOR NINJA COULD BE EXPECTED TO HANDLE.
SO MOST OF YOU...

...HAVING REACHED THAT SAME CONCLUSION...
...HAD ONLY ONE WAY OF RETAINING YOUR POINTS--BY CHEATING.

IN OTHER WORDS... WE SET UP THE TEST ON THE ASSUMPTION YOU'D CHEAT.
HMF.

AND, TO ENSURE THERE WOULD BE SUITABLE TARGETS FOR YOU TO CHEAT FROM, WE SNUCK IN A PAIR OF RINGERS...
...TWO JOURNEYMAN NINJA WHO ALREADY KNEW ALL THE ANSWERS.

WHAT?
!
AW, MAN!!!

IT TOOK ME FOREVER TO FIGURE OUT WHO THEY WERE!
OH, YEAH. ME TOO.
D'OH!
...

NA HA HA HA HA HA HA
HA HA HA! YEAH! IT WAS OBVIOUS!!!!

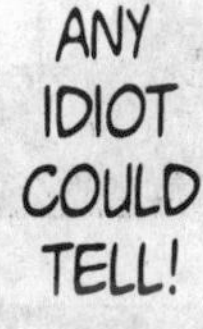
ANY IDIOT COULD TELL!

THAT FOOL... HE HAD NO IDEA.
RIGHT, HINATA?
R-RIGHT...

OF COURSE, ANYONE WHO CHEATED IN A CLUMSY OR OBVIOUS WAY....
RUSTLE RUSTLE
...FAILED.
!

FWUP

BECAUSE THERE MAY BE CIRCUMSTANCES WHERE BEING CAUGHT IN AN ACT OF ESPIONAGE CAN COST YOU MORE THAN JUST YOUR LIFE.

YOU PAY IN WAYS THAT CAN BE TAKEN FROM YOU LITTLE BY LITTLE, TIME AND TIME AGAIN, WHEN MANY LIVES HANG IN THE BALANCE.

BURN SCARS... PUNCTURES FROM WHERE SCREWS WERE USED... LONG SLASH MARKS...
HE'S BEEN TORTURED!!
ULP!

...!
GULP!

COOL... I BET HIS HANDS ARE EVEN WORSE!
BUT THAT'S WHAT HE GETS FOR BEING DUMB ENOUGH TO GET CAPTURED. IT'LL NEVER HAPPEN TO ME!

RUSTLE RUSTLE
THE INFORMATION YOU OBTAIN CAN'T BE TRUSTED...
...IF YOU CAN'T KEEP YOUR PRESENCE SECRET FROM THE ENEMY.

...

LEARN THAT AND LEARN IT WELL.
IF YOU BRING BACK INTELLIGENCE FROM A SUSPECT SOURCE OR A COMPROMISED OPERATION...
... YOU'RE DOING YOUR ENEMIES' WORK FOR THEM, PUTTING THOSE YOU SERVE IN DANGER.

THAT IS WHY WE MANEUVERED YOU INTO USING YOUR ESPIONAGE SKILLS TO CHEAT.
IT WAS THE QUICKEST WAY OF WEEDING OUT THE STUDENTS WHOSE SKILLS AREN'T YET UP TO SNUFF.

...
OKAY... BUT WHAT WAS THE DEAL WITH THE TENTH QUESTION?

YANK!

AH! THE TENTH QUESTION...
...WAS THE FIRST REAL TEST ON THE EXAM.

?

...
WHAT ON EARTH DO YOU MEAN?

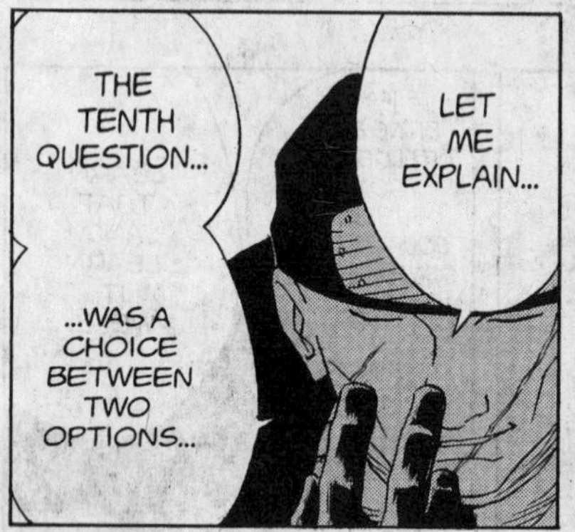
LET ME EXPLAIN...
THE TENTH QUESTION...
...WAS A CHOICE BETWEEN TWO OPTIONS...

...THAT WERE BOTH DIFFICULT AND DANGEROUS.
THOSE WHO CHOSE TO REJECT WERE FAILED, AND THEIR FRIENDS ALONG WITH THEM. THOSE WHO CHOSE TO ACCEPT AND COULDN'T ANSWER THE QUESTION...

... LOST ANY CHANCE OF EVER EVEN TRYING AGAIN.
IT WAS A NASTY, UNFAIR, NO-WIN SET OF OPTIONS.

LET'S SUPPOSE YOU ALL GO ON TO SUCCESSFULLY ATTAIN THE RANK OF *CHÛNIN.*
SO WHY DID I PRESENT THEM?

...

YOU MAY HAVE TO CROSS A TERRITORY THAT HAS BEEN HEAVILY MINED AND SET WITH TRAPS.
NOW... DO YOU ACCEPT YOUR MISSION? OR DO YOU REJECT IT...

YOU ARE ASSIGNED TO STEAL A VITAL ENEMY DOCUMENT...
...KNOWING NOTHING ABOUT THE SKILLS, DEPLOYMENT, OR MILITARY PREPAREDNESS OF YOUR FOE.

OF COURSE NOT!

COULD ANY *CHÛNIN* GET AWAY WITH ONLY TAKING ON THE SAFE JOBS?
...RATHER THAN PLACE YOUR OWN LIFE--OR THE LIVES OF YOUR COMPANIONS--IN JEOPARDY?
...

NO MATTER HOW DANGEROUS THE RISK...
...THERE WILL BE MISSIONS THAT YOU CANNOT DECLINE.

A NINJA MUST DEMONSTRATE VALOR THAT INSPIRES THOSE AROUND HIM...
...HELPING ALL TO OVERCOME THEIR FEAR.

THIS IS THE TALENT THAT WE MOST VALUE IN THE COMMANDER OF A *CHÛNIN* CELL!

THOSE WHO CAN'T GAMBLE WITH THEIR OWN FATE...
...WHO WOULD TRADE TODAY'S CERTAIN RISK FOR TOMORROW'S UNCERTAIN FUTURE...

... NEVER TAKING THE CHANCE THAT LIES BEFORE THEM...

...ARE WEAKLINGS WHO MAKE ONLY WEAK AND EASY DECISIONS.
IN MY OPINION, THEY DON'T BELONG IN THE RANKS OF THE *CHÛNIN* AT ALL!

ME!!!
BY CHOOSING TO ACCEPT...
THUMP
THUMPITY
...YOU ANSWERED THE ALMOST-INSOLUBLE TENTH QUESTION CORRECTLY.
IF YOU KEEP THAT SPIRIT, YOU CAN PROBABLY CONQUER ALL OF THE MANY DOUBTS AND DIFFICULTIES YOU'LL FACE.

YOU'VE PASSED THE FIRST HURDLE. PART ONE OF THE *CHÛNIN* SELECTION EXAM IS NOW CONCLUDED.
I'LL PRAY YOU FIGHT THE GOOD FIGHT!

YEAH. YOU DO THAT! GO PRAY!
HO HO...
AN ENTERTAINING KID...

!!
WHA-?!!
SHUK
SHUK

SLAP
SHHHHMMMM
STAB
WH- WHAT THE--

Newly Arrived
Secon chief
fficer

NONE OF YOU ARE IN ANY POSITION TO CELEBRATE.

I AM THE SECOND CHIEF EXAMINATION OFFICER..

...MITARASHI ANKO!!

TIME'S A-WASTIN', PEOPLE. LET'S GO!!

SHHHHNNNN
...?!

FOLLOW ME!!!

...

THIS NEW OFFICER ALMOST REMINDS ME...
...OF NARUTO.

RUSTLE
PSST
CAN'T YOU SENSE THE MOOD IN HERE?

SEVENTY-EIGHT OF YOU ARE STILL HERE?!
IBIKI! YOU PASSED TWENTY-SIX TEAMS?!

OBVIOUSLY YOU WENT WAY TOO EASY ON THEM.

THIS YEAR...
...WE HAVE APPLICANTS OF EXCEPTIONAL CALIBER.

YEAH, RIGHT.
I'LL CUT DOWN THE NUMBER BY HALF BEFORE THE NEXT TEST IS DONE.

!!
CUT US DOWN...
BY HALF?!

OOH! I GET CHARGED UP JUST THINKING ABOUT IT!
I'LL EXPLAIN THINGS IN DETAIL AS SOON AS WE MOVE TO OUR NEXT LOCATION... SO FOLLOW ME!!

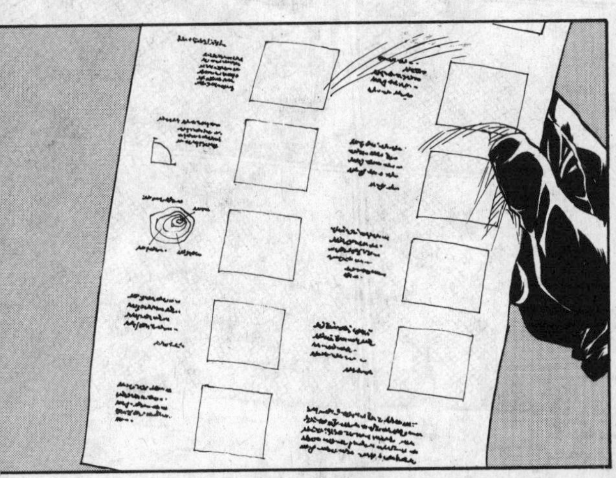

!

UZUMAKI NARUTO... ...IS A VERY INTRIGUING YOUNG MAN.
HE'S THE KIND OF PERSON WHO THINKS HE CAN PASS THE EXAM... WITH A COMPLETELY BLANK ANSWER SHEET.
HUH.

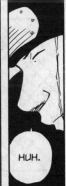

NO
TRESPASSING

GULP

THIS IS THE ARENA FOR THE SECOND EXAM: TRAINING GROUND 44.
ALSO KNOWN AS... THE **FOREST OF DEATH!!**

KISHIMOTO MASASHI'S "I ONLY SHOW YOU THESE THINGS SO YOU'LL UNDERSTAND HOW MUCH I LOVE MANGA" REJECTS CORNER...

THE ROUGH SKETCHES ABOVE SHOW HOW I LAY OUT THE VISUAL FLOW OF AN ACTION SEQUENCE. I TRY TO BE VERY CONSCIOUS OF THE FLOW OF SCENES IN NARUTO, SO AS SOON AS I COME UP WITH AN IDEA FOR AN ACTION SEQUENCE, I CHOREOGRAPH IT IN A SET OF THUMBNAIL DRAWINGS, LIKE STORYBOARDS. I TRY TO KEEP THE OVERALL PAGE COUNT FOR THE CHAPTER IN MIND, BUT THINGS USUALLY KEEP EXPANDING AND OPENING OUT, TAKING UP MORE AND MORE PAGES, WHILE I WORK OUT THE BEST CAMERA ANGLES, WITHOUT EVEN A THOUGHT TO WHERE THE DIALOGUE WILL FALL. NEXT I NUMBER THE SKETCHES, FIGURE OUT WHICH SCENES ARE THE MOST CRUCIAL, MAKE SURE THE TWO-PAGE SPREADS WILL ACTUALLY LAND ON PAGES THAT FACE EACH OTHER... AND THEN I NUMBER THE PAGES AND BREAK THEM DOWN INTO PANELS. THEN I DISCOVER I'VE USED UP MORE PAGES THAN I'M SUPPOSED TO HAVE IN THE ENTIRE CHAPTER... WHICH MEANS I HAVE TO GO BACK AND CUT SEQUENCES AND ERASE THINGS... CRYING LIKE A BABY ALL THE WHILE. YOU KNOW...

IT JUST OCCURRED TO ME...

THIS MAY BE WHY MY SCRIPTS ARE ALWAYS SO LATE!

Number 45: The Second Exam

...
...
IT LOOKS LIKE A PRETTY CREEPY PLACE.
HEH HEH ...

YOU'RE ABOUT TO FIND OUT FIRSTHAND...
...WHY THEY CALL THIS THE "FOREST OF DEATH"!

SULK

"OOO, YOU'RE ABOUT TO FIND OUT FIRSTHAND..."
"...WHY THEY CALL THIS THE 'FOREST OF DEATH'!"
VA-VOOM

LIKE THAT'S REALLY GONNA SCARE US.
YOU'RE TRYING TO PSYCH US OUT, AND I'M NOT GONNA FALL FOR IT!!

OH, REALLY?
YOU'RE PRETTY COCKY, HUH?
GRIN

SHING
FWAP

SHF
!
TAK

SLICE
!!
HEH. YOUR KIND ARE ALWAYS THE FIRST TO GO.
SHM

!!
SPILLING ALL THAT RICH, RED, LOVELY, LUSCIOUS BLOOD...
LAP...
PLIT
PE
SWI

YOUR KUNAI KNIFE...
I BELIEVE YOU DROPPED IT.
SHLUGK
GEE... THANKS.

READ THIS WAY

DON'T JUST STAND BEHIND ME...
...RADIATING BLOODLUST...

...UNLESS YOU'RE IN A HURRY TO DIE.
SMEK
SLUP

I'LL TRY TO KEEP IT UNDER CONTROL... BUT THE SIGHT OF WARM, FRESH BLOOD REALLY MAKES ME CRAZY...
...AND I WAS ALREADY REVVED UP... FROM LOSING A STRAND OF MY PRECIOUS HAIR.
SHLUGK

WE'VE GOT A REAL NUT-CASE PROCTORING THIS EXAM!
NOT GOOD. NOT GOOD AT ALL.

SORRY ABOUT THAT.
AND THIS OTHER GUY...
WHAT'S UP WITH THE BIG, FREAKISH TONGUE?
SHHF

* THE CHARACTER ON THE LOINCLOTH READS "CRIME."

LOOKS LIKE WE HAVE A HOT-BLOODED TEAM ON OUR HANDS THIS TIME OUT!
HEH... SHOULD BE FUN...
GRIN

WE'RE HOT-BLOODED... AND SHE'S BLOOD-THIRSTY!

BEFORE WE BEGIN THE SECOND EXAM...
...THERE'S SOMETHING I HAVE TO HAND OUT.

THEY'RE CONSENT FORMS. EVERYBODY HAS TO SIGN ONE.
...WHY?

WE WANT ALL THE DETAILS COVERED BEFORE THE FIRST DEATHS OCCUR.
SIGN BEFORE YOU GO IN, SO WE CAN'T BE HELD LIABLE.
YOU WOULDN'T WANT ME TO GET IN TROUBLE, WOULD YOU?♡
HA
HA
HA!

FIRST, I'LL EXPLAIN WHAT THE SECOND EXAM ENTAILS.

THEN YOU CAN SIGN THE FORMS.

WITH THE OTHER TWO MEMBERS OF YOUR CELL, BRING THE FORMS TO THE HUT BEHIND YOU AND SUBMIT THEM.

GOT THAT?
NOW, ABOUT THE EXAM.
TO PUT IT SIMPLY...

...IT'S A NO-HOLDS-BARRED SURVIVAL TEST.
!

SURVIVAL, EH?
ANOTHER PAIN-IN-THE-NECK EXAM! BLEAH!
FLAP

LET'S START WITH THE TOPOGRAPHY OF THIS TRAINING GROUND.
I'LL EXPLAIN THE REST LATER.
FWUP

TRAINING GROUND #44...
...IS BORDERED BY A CIRCULAR PERIMETER, INTERRUPTED AT REGULAR INTERVALS BY FORTY-FOUR LOCKED GATES.
44 LOCKED ENTRANCES
THERE ARE FORESTS AND A RIVER... AND IN THE CENTER IS A TOWER...
...ABOUT TEN KILOMETERS FROM THOSE GATES.
RIVER
APPROXIMATELY 10 KM
TOWER
TRAINING GROUND #44
TRAINING GROUND #43

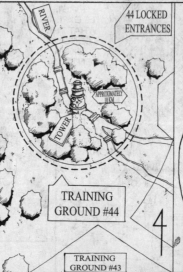

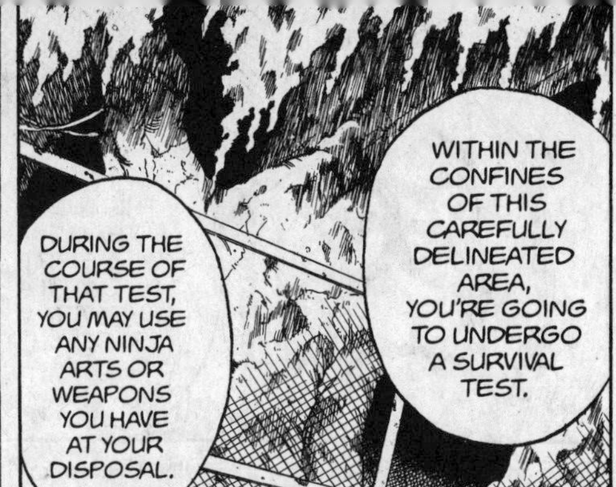

WITHIN THE CONFINES OF THIS CAREFULLY DELINEATED AREA, YOU'RE GOING TO UNDERGO A SURVIVAL TEST.
DURING THE COURSE OF THAT TEST, YOU MAY USE ANY NINJA ARTS OR WEAPONS YOU HAVE AT YOUR DISPOSAL.

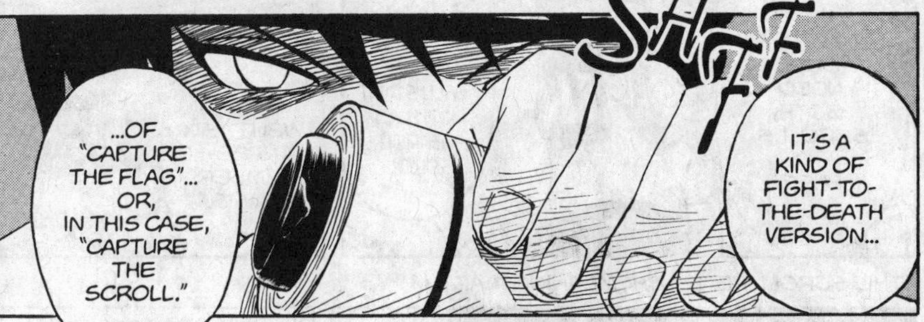

SHFF
IT'S A KIND OF FIGHT-TO-THE-DEATH VERSION...
...OF "CAPTURE THE FLAG"... OR, IN THIS CASE, "CAPTURE THE SCROLL."

SCROLL?
EXACTLY!

SHF
THERE'S A "SCROLL OF HEAVEN" AND A "SCROLL OF EARTH" ...AND YOUR OBJECTIVE IS TO ACQUIRE BOTH SCROLLS.
天
地

THAT'S TWENTY-SIX THREE-MEMBER TEAMS.

*THIS SCROLL READS *TEN*, MEANING "HEAVEN."

...AND THE OTHER THIRTEEN WILL START WITH AN EARTH SCROLL.

BUT YOU'LL NEED BOTH SCROLLS TO PASS.

*THIS SCROLL READS *CHI*, MEANING "EARTH."

SO YOUR OBJECTIVE IS TO HOLD ON TO YOUR OWN SCROLL, GET YOUR HANDS ON ONE OF THE OTHER KIND...

...AND THEN BRING THEM BOTH...
...TO THE TOWER AT THE CENTER.

IN OTHER WORDS, AT LEAST HALF OF US--
--THE THIRTEEN TEAMS WHOSE SCROLLS ARE STOLEN--WILL FAIL.
YOU BET! AND THERE'S A TIME LIMIT!
YOU HAVE 120 HOURS IN WHICH TO COMPLETE THIS EXAM--
--EXACTLY FIVE DAYS!

FIVE DAYS?!
WHAT ARE WE SUPPOSED TO DO FOR FOOD?!
THAT'S YOUR PROBLEM.
THE FORESTS ARE FULL OF NATURE'S BOUNTY.
OF COURSE, THEY'RE ALSO FULL OF MAN-EATING ANIMALS, DEADLY INSECTS, AND POISONOUS PLANTS.

THERE'S NO WAY AS MANY AS THIRTEEN TEAMS WILL PASS THIS.
SIGH
AS THE TIME SHORTENS, THE TRIALS WILL COME HARDER AND FASTER...
...WITH LESS RECOVERY TIME FOR ANY MISTAKES, ACCIDENTS, OR INJURIES.
YOU'LL BE SURROUNDED BY ENEMIES AT ALL TIMES, SO YOU'LL HAVE TO SLEEP WITH ONE EYE OPEN.

SO, IN ADDITION TO THOSE WHO DIE IN ATTEMPTS TO DEFEND OR CAPTURE A SCROLL...
...SOME OF YOU ARE BOUND TO SUCCUMB TO EXHAUSTION, EXPOSURE, STARVATION, AND DEHYDRATION.

WAVE
NOW LET'S TALK ABOUT THE RULES... AND WHAT OFFENSES YOU CAN BE DISQUALIFIED FOR!

OBVIOUSLY, THE TEAMS THAT FAIL TO REACH THE TOWER IN TIME--
--AS A THREE-MEMBER CELL, CARRYING BOTH A HEAVEN AND AN EARTH SCROLL-- ARE OUT.

SO IS ANY TEAM THAT LOSES A MEMBER, WHETHER TO DEATH OR TO SEVERE INJURY.

AND UNDER NO CIRCUM-STANCES...
...CAN YOU LEAVE THE FOREST BEFORE THE TIME IS UP.
NO RECESS. NO TIME-OUTS.

ALSO...
...YOU'RE FORBIDDEN TO LOOK AT THE CONTENTS OF THE SCROLLS UNTIL YOU'RE INSIDE THE TOWER!

WHAT HAPPENS IF WE SNEAK A PEEK?

THAT'S FOR THOSE WHO LOOK TO KNOW! ♡

?
IF ANY OF YOU MAKE IT TO THE *CHÛNIN* LEVEL, THERE WILL BE TIMES WHEN YOU'LL BE ENTRUSTED WITH TOP-SECRET DOCUMENTS...
...SO CONSIDER THIS A TEST OF YOUR TRUSTWORTHI-NESS.

WE'LL TRADE ONE SCROLL FOR EVERY THREE FORMS.
WHEN YOU'VE GOT YOURS, CHOOSE THE GATE YOU WANT TO START FROM. EVERYONE WILL BEGIN AT THE SAME TIME.
THAT'S ALL THE EXPLANATION YOU GET.

ONE FINAL PIECE OF ADVICE...
STAY ALIVE!

IT'S ALMOST TIME TO DISTRIBUTE THE SCROLLS.

SHF

SKF

SMART! TO KEEP US IN THE DARK...
...THEY'RE CONCEALING WHICH TYPE OF SCROLL EACH TEAM GETS... AND WHICH MEMBER IS CARRYING IT!

IT'S JUST LIKE THAT GUY IBIKI SAID...
...STEALING INTELLIGENCE IS A MATTER OF LIFE AND DEATH!

EVERYONE IS AN ENEMY!!

AND WE'RE PROBABLY ALL EQUALLY DETERMINED.
IF WE'RE ALL WILLING TO FIGHT TO THE DEATH, THIS COULD BECOME A MASSACRE.
CONSENT FORM

HEH HEH...
IT'S FINALLY STARTING TO SINK IN... WHY WE WANT THOSE CONSENT FORMS!

A FIGHT TO THE DEATH? WHAT A NUISANCE... BUT IF IT'S THE ONLY WAY...
...LOOKS LIKE NARUTO'S OUR TARGET.
GRUMBLE
GATE 27
• SHIKAMARU
• CHOJI • INO

WOOHOO! IF IT'S SURVIVAL SKILLS THEY WANT, WE'VE GOT IT MADE!
DON'T GO SOFT ON US, HINATA!
...
GATE 16
• KIBA
• HINATA • SHINO

HEH HEH... THE TIME HAS FINALLY COME...
...TO CARRY OUT OUR ORDERS IN THE OPEN.
GATE 20
OTONIN
(SOUND) TEAM

YEAH! YEAH! WE CAN'T LOSE, I TELL YA!!
ANYONE COMES NEAR US, I'LL KILL 'EM MYSELF!
OH, PLEASE!
STAB
GATE 12
NARUTO'S TEAM

I'VE GOT TO LOOK OUT FOR ENEMY TEAMS...
...BUT FIVE DAYS IN THE FOREST WITH THAT CREEPY GAARA... ARRRGH!
GATE 6
• GAARA
• KANKURO
• TEMARI

GATE 38
KABUTO'S TEAM

TARGET THE ROOKIES FIRST.

IT LOOKS LIKE WE'VE GOT CARTE BLANCHE TO PICK THEM OFF FROM HERE ON IN...

...WHICH SHOULD MAKE OUR JOB A LOT EASIER.

GATE 15 THE MYSTERIOUS KUSANIN GRASS NINJA TRIO.

*THE TAGS ON THE HATS READ (RIGHT TO LEFT) "CRIME," "EVIL," AND "PUNISHMENT."

GATE 41
• NEJI
• LEE • TENTEN
MASTER GUY, I WILL DO MY BEST!

SLAP

ALL RIGHT, EVERYONE, FOLLOW YOUR PROCTORS TO YOUR RESPECTIVE GATES!
WHEN THE SIGNAL SOUNDS IN HALF AN HOUR, THE EXAM WILL BEGIN!!

CLICK

12

NOW!!
PART TWO OF THE JOURNEYMAN NINJA SELECTION EXAM BEGINS...
KATCH
THOSE THREE, RIGHT?
GO FOR THE BRATS!
TAK TAK TAK
ALL RIGHT!!
ONN N
LET'S GO!!

NARUTO

岸本斉史

Lately, all over the world, there has been an upswing in terrorist acts—attacks by armed groups and the taking of hostages—by the worst kind of criminals. In an effort to resolve these situations with as little bloodshed and fanfare as possible, nations all over the globe are increasingly turning toward special operations forces, armed with the latest technologies and finely honed skills, giving them superlative intelligence-gathering capabilities. Such operatives are truly the modern analog to the type of warriors who, in the past, were known as ninja!

—Masashi Kishimoto, 2001

NARUTO

VOL. 6

SAKURA'S DECISION

STORY AND ART BY

MASASHI KISHIMOTO

SAKURA サクラ

Smart and studious, Sakura is the brightest of Naruto's classmates, but she's constantly distracted by her crush on Sasuke. Her goal: to win Sasuke's heart!

NARUTO ナルト

When Naruto was born, a destructive fox spirit was imprisoned inside his body. Spurned by the older villagers, he's grown into an attention-seeking troublemaker. His goal: to become the village's next *Hokage*.

SASUKE サスケ

The top student in Naruto's class, Sasuke comes from the prestigious Uchiha clan. His goal: to get revenge on a mysterious person who wronged him in the past.

MITARASHI ANKO
みたらしアンコ

The Second Chief Examination Officer, responsible for the portion of the exam that takes place in the Forest of Death! She's determined to cut down the number of teams by half before the next segment of the test is complete, and she seems to relish the thought of watching the students go down in flames.

ROCK LEE ロック・リー

Rock Lee, a devoted disciple of his teacher, Master Gai, is one of the most talented young shinobi around, and he's completely infatuated with Sakura.

THE SOUND NINJA (OTONIN) 音忍

Are these mysterious ninja roaming the forest in search of their second scroll, or something else entirely?

THE ASUMA CELL
Choji チョウジ
Ino いの
Shikamaru シカマル

Sakura's rival Ino and her team hope to steal their second scroll from the weakest team in the bunch—Naruto's!

THE STORY SO FAR...

Twelve years ago, a destructive nine-tailed fox spirit attacked the ninja village of Konohagakure. The *Hokage*, or village champion, defeated the fox by sealing its soul into the body of a baby boy. Now that boy, Uzumaki Naruto, has grown up to become a ninja-in-training, learning the art of *ninjutsu* with his classmates Sakura and Sasuke.

Astonishingly, Naruto and his team passed the written section of the Chûnin (Journeyman Ninja) Selection Exam, but they face new dangers in the exam's second portion, which is conducted in the Forest of Death! The object of the exercise is to reach the tower in the center of the forest with two scrolls in hand, and all three team members alive, before five days elapse. Each of the 26 teams is given only one scroll, and must steal the second scroll from another team using any means necessary!

VOL. 6

SAKURA'S DECISION

CONTENTS

Number 46: The Password Is...

HOP
POP

THE TOWER'S WHERE EVERYONE IS ULTIMATELY GOING...

POP
SHF

TAK
SHF

...SO WE MIGHT AS WELL SET TRAPS AS CLOSE TO THERE AS POSSIBLE.

SNIFF
SNIFF
SNIFF
!!

FOUND THEM ALREADY, HUH?
WHERE ARE THEY?

STUPID KIDS... THEY MIGHT AS WELL BE SHOUTING, "CAPTURE US!"
FROM THE SOUND OF THINGS, THEY KNOW WE'RE SOMEWHERE NEARBY...
...BUT THEY HAVEN'T FIGURED OUT WHERE YET.

SHIVER
!

WHAT'S WRONG? YOU'RE AS WHITE AS A SHEET.
AGH!

!!

SQUIRM
SHLUK
WHAT **IS** THAT THING?!

!!
PLOP
PLOP
PLOP
PLOP
PLOP

AAAAAGH!!
SPLAT
SPLAT
SPLAT

GROSS...
SHUF
!

EEYOOO...
ICK...
SLUP

HUNH?!
TWANG

THE FLYING LEECHES OF KONOHA VILLAGE CAN SENSE PERSPIRATION AND BODY HEAT AND FLING THEMSELVES EN MASSE!
IF YOU CAN'T GET THEM OFF YOUR BODY WITHIN FIVE MINUTES, YOU'RE FINISHED. AND IF YOU PANIC TRYING TO GET AWAY FROM THEM... WELL...
ONE TEAM DOWN!

HELP!!!
SWOOP

AAAAGH!

WELL...
...THAT WAS FAST!

...!!
DID YOU GUYS HEAR SOMEONE... SCREAM?

THIS PLACE IS CREEPING ME OUT!
I'M TELLING YOU, SAKURA, IT'S NO BIG DEAL.

...

NOT IN FRONT OF ME, BOZO! I'M A LADY!
USE THE BUSHES!!!
IF IT WERE SASUKE, ON THE OTHER HAND... HEH HEH HEH...
INNER SAKURA
WHAP
OW!!

...UHHH... I GOTTA TAKE A LEAK...
GRUNT
GRUNT
!!

OH, MAN! WHAT A RELIEF! FEELIN' GOOD NOW!
!

I TOLD YOU, YOU'RE IN THE PRESENCE OF A LADY! DON'T BE VUL--
SIZZLE

SLAM
S-SASUKE... I APPRECIATE THE CHIVALRY, BUT THAT WAS WAY OVER THE TOP!
WHAT THE--?!
!!
SWIPE
WH-WHAT WAS THAT FOR?!!
WHAT HAVE YOU DONE WITH NARUTO?
UM. WHAT?
HELLO!
I'M RIGHT IN FRONT OF YOU... BLEEDING!
YOU'RE WEARING YOUR SHURIKEN THROWING STARS ON YOUR LEFT THIGH. NARUTO'S RIGHT-HANDED.
AND YOU FORGOT THE CUT THAT NARUTO GOT FROM THE PROCTOR JUST BEFORE THE EXAM.
YOU'RE EVEN WORSE AT DISGUISE SPELLS THAN THE REAL NARUTO.
!!

POP
SINCE YOU'VE FORCED ME TO COME CLEAN, WHY DON'T YOU DO THE SAME?
WHICH ONE OF YOU TWO HAS THE SCROLL?!

UNFORTUNATELY, YOU'VE FORCED ME TO BE DIRECT!
SHM

TAK TAK

VNN

FWOOSH

FIRE STYLE! ART OF THE PHOENIX FLOWER... THE TOUCH-ME-NOT!

FWP FWP FW

TIGER

WHOP
WHOP
HOP
WHOP
CHING
HOP
!
SASUKE!!
SQUIRM
THAT IDIOT...
YEAH!!
THUK
YOU LEFT AN OPENING-- LUCKY ME!!
WHIP
WHIP
THOK
THOK
THOK
FWP
THOK
HAH!

!!
SIZZLE
A LETTER BOMB!
BOOOOOOM
OW!
TH UD
BETTER AND BETTER. ONE FALSE MOVE, AND I'LL KILL YOU.
NOW HAND OVER THE SCROLL!
SASUKE!!
....!!

HEH...
!!
CHAK
!!
FWOOM!!
YOU'RE NOT GETTING AWAY THAT EASY!
CHAKRA ENERGY WILL HOLD THIS TO THE SOLE OF MY SHOE...
LATE AS USUAL, NARUTO!!
HMMM

SHINK
!!
KA
CHK
GAAH!!!
SHOO
TAK
M
!!
THOM

DLIT PLIT

SASUKE...
HE GAVE ME NO CHOICE! NOW MOVE! WE DON'T KNOW WHERE HIS FRIENDS ARE!

YOU GOT THAT?
KEEP STANDING THERE, AND YOU'LL END UP DEAD!!!

GAA
MY... ARM!
THIS IS AWFUL!
OHHH!
!
SHLUP
I THOUGHT COMING ALONE WOULD HELP CONCEAL MY PRESENCE... INSTEAD, IT'S BEEN MY RUIN!

LEAP
LEAP
SIGH
GONE...

REMEMBER THIS. IF WE GET SEPARATED AGAIN...
...WE CAN'T TRUST EACH OTHER BLINDLY!
IT COULD END UP THE WAY THIS DID!

BUT WHAT CAN WE DO?

THE SAFEST THING IS FOR US TO HAVE A SECRET PASSWORD.
THAT WAY, WE'LL KNOW. NO MATTER WHO THEY LOOK LIKE OR HOW THEY SOUND, IF ONE OF US GETS THAT WRONG...
...THEY'RE AN ENEMY!

LISTEN VERY CAREFULLY. I'LL SAY IT ONLY ONCE!

IT'S A POEM CALLED "NINKI"--"NINJA OPPORTUNITY."
WHEN I ASK FOR IT, HERE'S WHAT YOU RESPOND...

"WE THRIVE IN THE CHAOS OF THE ENEMY TIDE. QUIET *SHINOBI* DON'T NEED DENS TO HIDE.
"OUR ONLY CONCERN IS TO WATCH AND WAIT...

"...UNTIL THE ENEMY LOWERS THE GATE."
...
BINGO!

AND YOU EXPECT ME TO REMEMBER THAT... **HOW?!**
YOU ARE SUCH A DUNCE. I'VE ALREADY GOT IT DOWN!

VERY GOOD. TIME TO PULL BACK AND REGROUP...

WE NEED A BETTER PASSWORD! HOW ABOUT "SWORDFISH"?
I'LL TAKE THE SCROLL.

FWOOOM

WHAT THE...?

FWUM
!
OW!

!!
A NEW ENEMY?!
YAAAAAH!!
BOOOM

BABOOOOM

STICK AROUND, YOU TWO. IT COULD BE FUN!
I'LL GO IN ALONE!

!

SAKURA...
SASUKE!
WHIRL

STAY BACK! DON'T COME NEAR!
WHAT'S THE PASSWORD?
THE "NINKI."
FWD

OH! RIGHT!
"WE THRIVE IN THE CHAOS OF THE ENEMY TIDE. QUIET *SHINOBI* DON'T NEED DENS TO HIDE. OUR ONLY CONCERN IS TO WATCH AND WAIT UNTIL THE ENEMY LOWERS THE GATE."
GOOD!

YOW... ARE YOU GUYS ALL RIGHT?
!!
!!

NOT SO FAST, NARUTO! THE PASSWORD?
RIGHT. "NINKI."
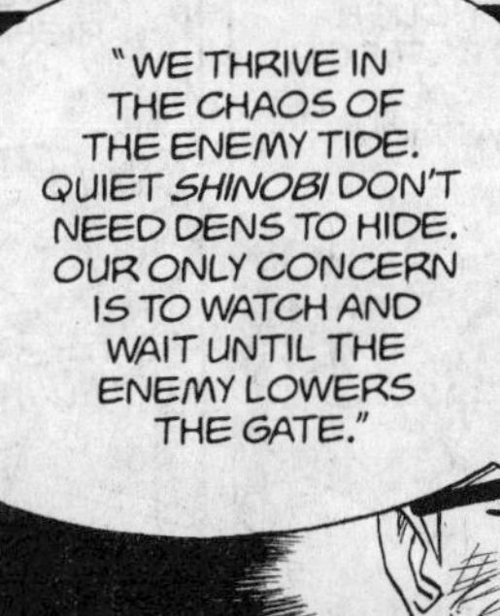
"WE THRIVE IN THE CHAOS OF THE ENEMY TIDE. QUIET *SHINOBI* DON'T NEED DENS TO HIDE. OUR ONLY CONCERN IS TO WATCH AND WAIT UNTIL THE ENEMY LOWERS THE GATE."

!!

FWIP

TOK

HEYY!

WHAT?!

!!

WHAT ARE YOU DOING, SASUKE?
NARUTO GOT THE PASSWORD RIGHT!
WHUD

AND THIS TIME, HE'S GOOD ENOUGH TO DEFLECT MY ATTACK!
WAIT JUST A SECOND HERE!
TAK

HEH

WELL DONE!
HUH?
ONG

WHAT GAVE ME AWAY?

I KNEW YOU WERE UNDERGROUND, EAVESDROPPING ON EVERYTHING WE SAID.
THAT'S WHY I CHOSE THAT KIND OF PASSWORD...

...THE KIND THE REAL NARUTO WOULD NEVER MANAGE TO MEMORIZE.
GOTCHA, IMPOSTER!

I SEE...
WATCH AND WAIT, EH?
THIS IS GOING TO BE MORE FUN THAN I THOUGHT!

MEET KISHIMOTO MASASHI'S ASSISTANTS - PART ONE

° ASSISTANT NO. 1: TAKAHASHI KAZUHIRO

PROFILE

- A NATIVE OF KYUSHU WITH A TASTE FOR GOOD SAKE AND RED BEAN BUNS, HE COMES FROM THE BEAUTIFUL CITY OF BEPPU, ALSO KNOWN AS HELL (BECAUSE OF THE SULFUROUS FUMES THAT BILLOW FROM ITS FAMOUS HOT SPRINGS).
- LOVES TO EAT AND ALWAYS HAS HIS NOSE IN THE OFFICE REFRIGERATOR.
- LOTS OF TREASURES ARE SLEEPING IN HIS CLOSET AT HOME.
- HAS A TASTE FOR LEATHER AND WILD MOTORBIKE RIDES.
- HE'S A SUB-ZERO SUPER-COOL BAD BOY WHO LIKES TO PLAY DUMB. HE WORKS AS MY BETA -- THE ARTIST WHO SPOTS THE SOLID BLACKS IN HAIR AND CLOTHING, LAYS DOWN THE HALF-TONES, AND COMPLETES THE BACKGROUND ART -- AND LIVES LIKE A CHIEF.

UNH...
Number 47: Predator!!

FWP
OOH...

OHH...
MMPH...
OWW...

...!
HUNH?

...
WHERE'D SAKURA AND THAT BONE-HEAD SASUKE GO?
!!!

...
YAAAAH!
I-I-IT'S...

Number 47: Predator!!
HSSSS
...HUGE!!!

I-I'VE NEVER SEEN...
...A SNAKE THAT BIG!

WH-WHAT IS UP WITH THIS FOREST...?!
SSSLIDE

TAK

!!
GRRRRR

FWUP
BEHIND ME?!
ACK!

!!
...TH-THE TAIL...!!

SSSSS
!

GULP

AAAAAAGH!!

THAT WAS ANOTHER PHONY NARUTO!!

IF HE'D BEEN THE REAL THING...
...HE'D HAVE SAID SOMETHING LIKE, "WHAT'S THAT STUPID PASSWORD AGAIN?"

THIS SCROLL READS *CHI*, MEANING "EARTH."

WHERE IS THAT FOOL NARUTO, ANYWAY?
THIS ONE... GIVES ME THE CREEPS!

I SUPPOSE YOU'D LIKE TO STEAL OUR EARTH SCROLL, WOULDN'T YOU...?
...SINCE YOU'VE ALREADY GOT A HEAVEN SCROLL!
地
FWIP

GLUG

SLUPP

LICK
GULP
GULP
NOW... SHALL WE SEE...
...JUST WHO WILL BE STEALING SCROLLS FROM WHOM?

!!

WE'LL FIGHT TO THE DEATH!

PULSE

HUFF
PUFF
PUFF
...HE'S CASTING... AN ILLUSION!
THOK

UHHN...
BLORTCH!!

IT'S NOT... DEATH... JUST AN INCREDIBLE SIMULATION!
I LOOKED INTO HIS EYES... AND HE MADE ME FEEL IT... AND BELIEVE IT!
HUFF
PUFF
PUFF
PUFF

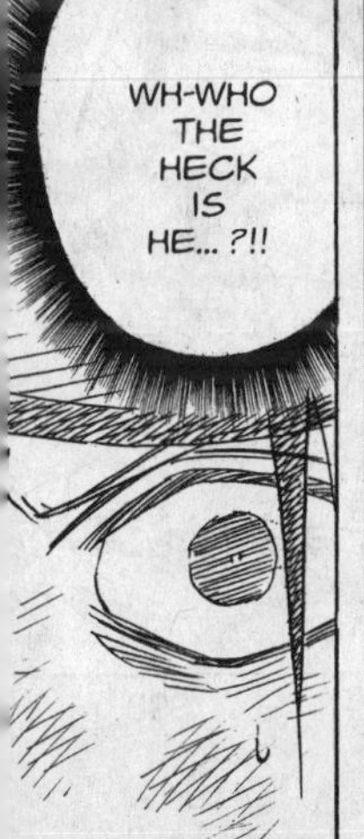
WH-WHO THE HECK IS HE...?!!

SAKURA...

!

...!!

CRUD! IF WE DON'T RETREAT NOW...
...WE'RE FINISHED!
THE ONLY OTHER OPTION IS DEATH!!
HEH... I IMAGINE YOU'RE PARALYZED BY NOW...

READ THIS WAY

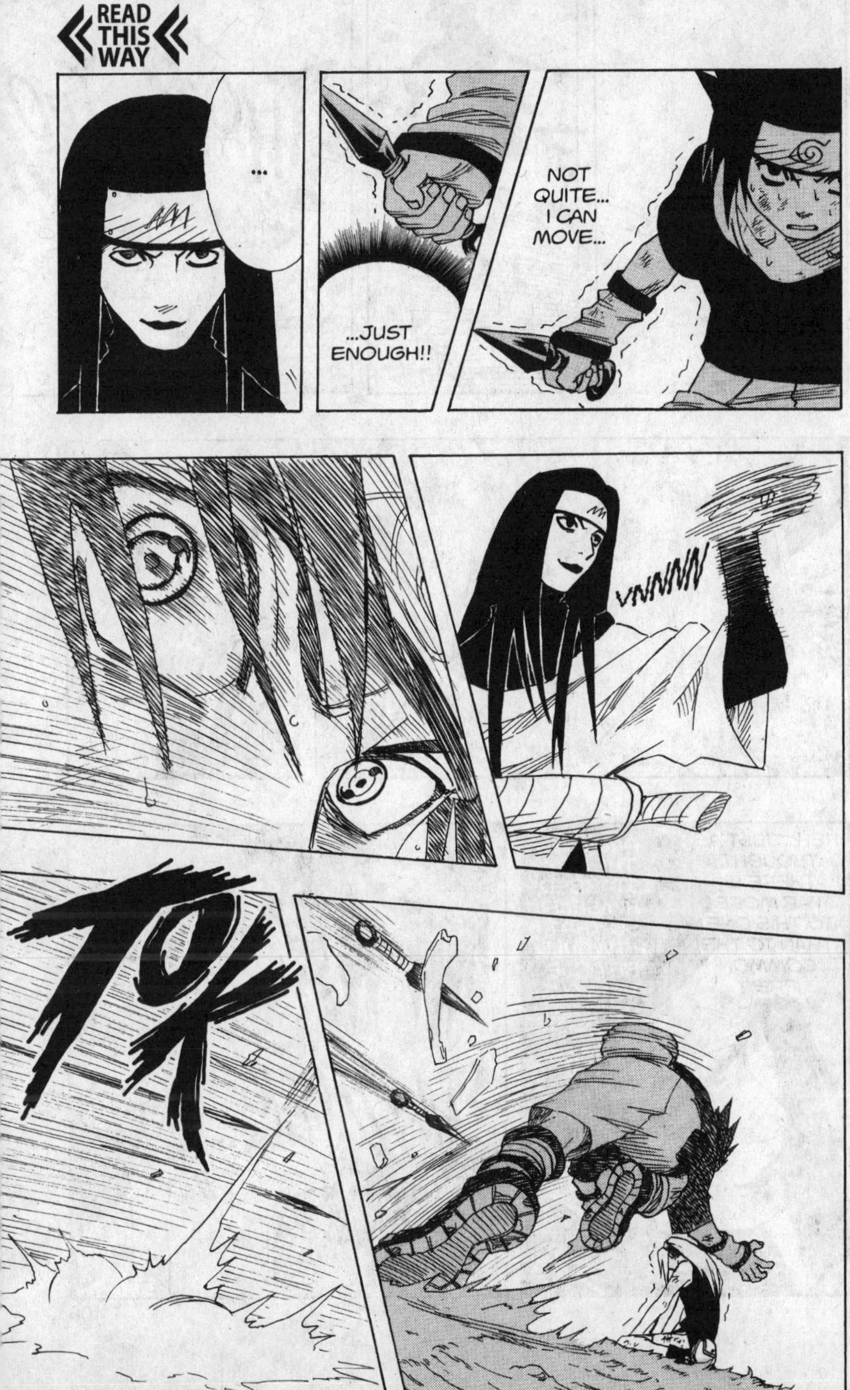

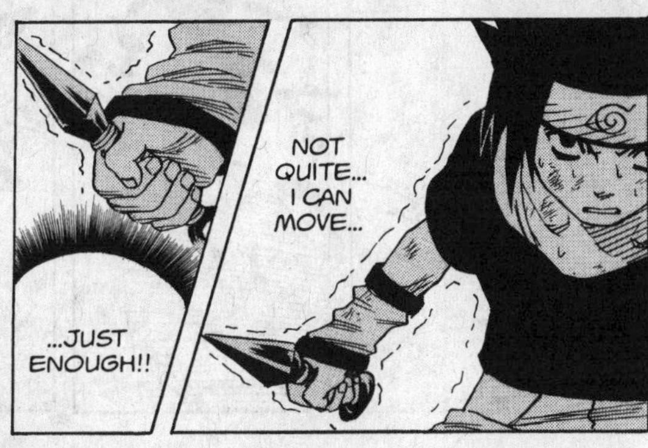
NOT QUITE... I CAN MOVE...
...JUST ENOUGH!!

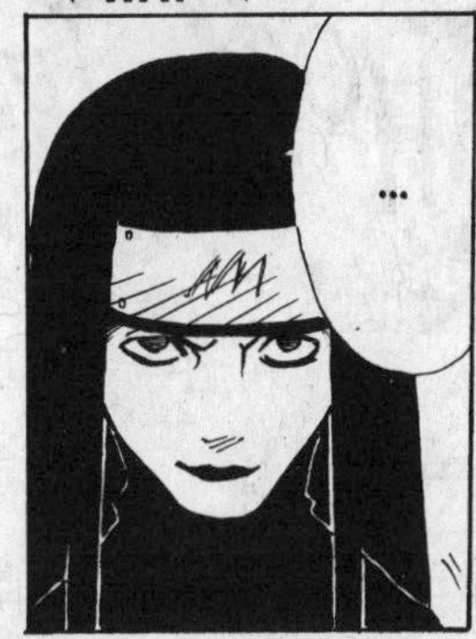
...

VNNNNN

THOK THOK

STAB

(HUFF)
(PUFF)
(PUFF)

UUNH...
SHLUUGK
!!

AMAZING! THE BOY STABBED HIMSELF SO THAT HE WOULD BE ABLE TO FOCUS ON THE PAIN AND BLOCK OUT FEAR AND ILLUSION!
HEH... JUST AS I THOUGHT, THERE IS FAR MORE TO THIS ONE THAN TO THE COMMON PREY!

Z
Z

HEY! HEY, YOU! OUT THERE! YOU BETTER SPIT ME OUT WHILE YOU'VE GOT THE CHANCE!!!

MORE, PLEASE. KEEP IT COMING!!
ULP!

BUT HOW DO I MAKE THIS FREAK BARF?
...

I GOTTA GET OUTTA HERE BEFORE MISTER SLIMY DIGESTS ME!
...RATS...!!

PUFF
THAT'S IT!!! ART OF THE DOPPEL-GANGER, SOLID FORM!!

SQUISH

I'M THE SHINOBI WHO'LL BECOME LORD HOKAGE. SO DON'T MESS WITH ME!!
(HUFF)
(PUFF)
I GOT BETTER THINGS TO DO WITH MY LIFE THAN END UP A BIG SNAKE TURD!
HUFF

RIGHT!!
NOW, TO FIND SAKURA AND SASUKE...!!

READ THIS WAY

SASUKE!
SNAAAAAKE!!

MMM....
MNNNNN!!!

HSSSSS

SSSLITHER
TAP

WHOA...
MY CHI IS SO OUT OF WHACK, I OVER-LOOKED A GIANT SNAKE!

THUK THUK THUK

W
MP

HUFF
PUFF
PUFF
SKKF

!
SHRED
SHRED

SSS
FOR SHAME, LETTING YOUR GUARD DOWN! STAY ON YOUR TOES, LIKE A GOOD PREY SHOULD!
LITHER
IT MAKES THE CHASE SO MUCH MORE REWARDING...

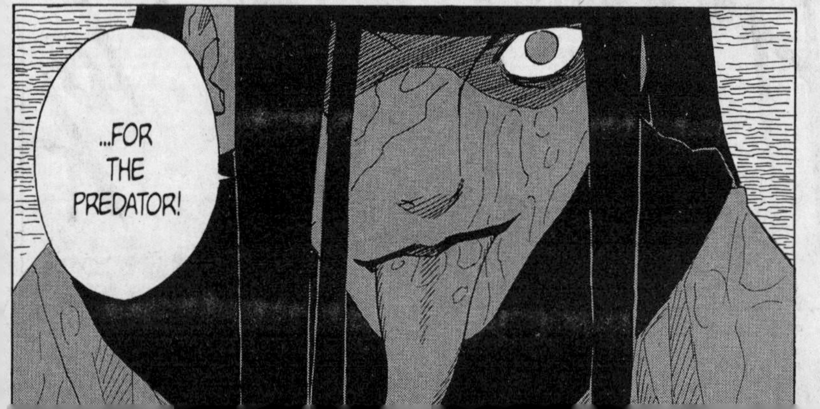
...FOR THE PREDATOR!

WHIIIP
SLITHER

CHUK CHUK
HOP

...
SORRY, SASUKE...

!

I CAN'T REMEMBER...
...THAT STUPID PASSWORD!
ONNNG

Number 48: The Target Is...!!

SWEET! NARUTO, THAT WAS AWESOME!!

NARUTO TO THE RESCUE, HUNH? YOU'RE COMPLETELY PSYCHED TO BE SAVING THE DAY... BUT...
...NOW WOULD BE A GOOD TIME TO RUN FOR YOUR LIFE!!!

THIS GUY IS WAY OUT OF OUR LEAGUE!!!

Number 48:
The Target Is...!!

HEH HEH... MY COMPLIMENTS ON YOUR STUNNING DEFEAT OF THE GIANT SNAKE...
...NARUTO.

!
THIS GUY'S A FREAK. HE'S A MAN... BUT ALL I CAN SEE WHEN I LOOK AT HIM IS A SNAKE. EVERYTHING ABOUT HIM...

SNAKEY!
GRRRR
I'LL BET THAT SNAKE WAS HIS!

EVERY TIME I EVER TRIED TO RESCUE US...
...HE'S MADE THINGS WORSE. BUT THERE MUST BE SOME WAY TO...

HEY!
WHY DON'T YOU PICK ON SOMEONE YOUR OWN SIZE...? OR SOMETHING LIKE THAT...

I'VE GOT TO STOP THIS BEFORE HE GETS US ALL KILLED.

THIS IS ALL I CAN THINK OF...

SNAP

!
OH... SHARIN-GAN MIMIC EYES... BUT HE STOPPED!

IF IT'S OUR SCROLL YOU WANT, COME AND GET IT!
SHF
JUST...
...TAKE IT AND GO!

!!
WHAT?!

HUH?

HEH...

SASUKE!! WHAT THE HECK DO YOU THINK YOU'RE DOING?!
IS THIS SOME CLEVER WAY OF BEATING THE ENEMY...? BY HANDING OVER EVERYTHING WE'VE GOT?!

WELL DONE...
YOU'RE OBVIOUSLY NATURAL-BORN PREY...
SSSLIDE

...INSTINCTIVELY KNOWING THAT YOUR ONLY HOPE...
...LIES IN THE CHANCE OF THE PREDATOR BEING DISTRACTED BY SOME TASTIER BAIT!

FLIP
COME AND GET IT!
TAP
FWUP

!!

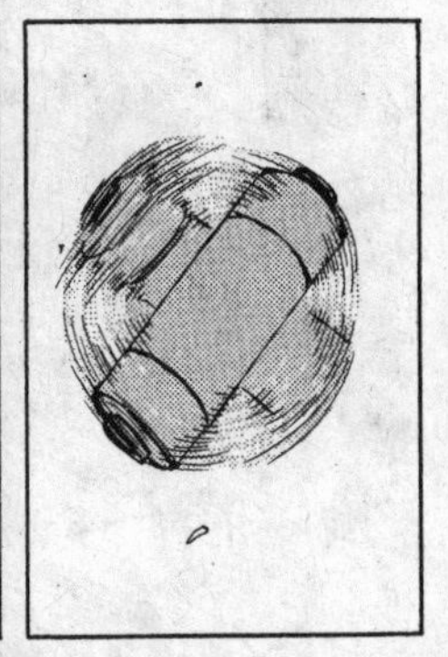

POK
!!

SKF

STAY OUT OF THIS!
YOU'LL RUIN EVERY-THING!!

POW
HUH?!

TAK

HUFF
PUFF
PUFF
PUFF
WHAT DO YOU THINK YOU'RE DOING?!
TAP

NARUTO... WHAT ARE YOU...?

I FORGOT THE STUPID PASSWORD...
SO I CAN'T PROVE IT...
!
BUT THIS SO-CALLED SASUKE IS OBVIOUSLY A FAKE!

WHAT?!

NARUTO...
...YOU IDIOT! I'M ME...!

...THAT'S BULL!

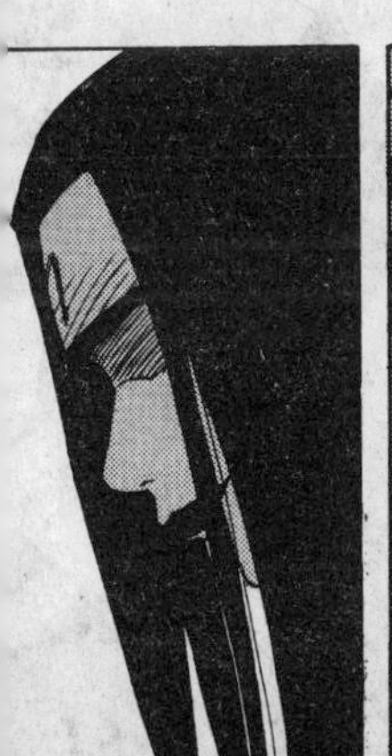

AND YOU'RE THE IDIOT, IDIOT!
HUFF
PUFF
PUFF
YOU'RE A COWARD. WHICH SASUKE ISN'T. SO YOU'RE NOT HIM!!!
I'M NOT SO SURE WE NEED TO BE AFRAID OF THIS GUY...
AND EVEN IF WE DID HAND OVER THE SCROLL... THERE'S NO GUARANTEE HE'D SPARE US!
SO, EVEN IF YOU WERE SASUKE, I'D STILL BE TELLING YOU YOU'RE AN IDIOT... AND MAYBE A CHICKEN, TOO!
...!
OH, NARUTO! THIS IS RICH!

AND YOU'RE RIGHT.

WHY BARGAIN...

SHF

...WHEN I CAN SIMPLY KILL YOU... AND TAKE THE SCROLL?
NIP

SLUP

SHUT UP!

TAK TAK

TAK

GRRR

AW, MAN...!

HOP

DON'T DO IT, NARUTO!!

ART OF THE FAMILIAR SPIRIT!
GNNNO

MY FAITH IN SASUKE IS TOTALLY SHOT!!!

ONNG

!!

POW
BAM BAM
NARUTO!!
WHAM
...OW...

GAH
K

LUB
DUB

SLLIP

EXCELLENT... BUT LET'S NOT TAKE CHANCES. EAT THE BOY! ♡
FWUUUP

LUB DUB

EAT SNOT, SUCKER!!
ONNNG
!!
HOW COULD THE BRAT POSSIBLY...?

READ THIS WAY

RRRROAR!!

NARUTO'S... COM-PLETELY SNAPPED... BUT...
WHERE DID HE GET THAT KIND OF POWER?!

!!
YAAH!
ONG
ONG

AGH!!
POW
LOOK AT THOSE EYES... HE'S...

...!!
IS THAT REALLY NARUTO...?!

HO HO... AND THE FUN HAS JUST BEGUN!

AND IT'S SASUKE'S TURN NEXT! HOW WILL HE TAKE IT?!

!!

SASUKE!!

POW

!!

...HEY, ARE YOU OKAY...?
PUFF
HUFF
PUFF
...!
...

LUB DUB

...YOU BIG CHICKEN?!
HUFF
PUFF

NARUTO

MEET KISHIMOTO MASASHI'S ASSISTANTS
PART TWO
ASSISTANT NO. 2: KAZISA OSAMU

100.11.8

KAZISA

HAPPY FIRST ANNIVERSARY!

PROFILE

- USUALLY WEARS GLASSES, BUT WHEN HE TAKES THEM OFF AND PUTS ON HIS CONTACTS HE BECOMES THE HANDSOME OFFICE HEARTTHROB. NO, REALLY!
- HE FALLS ASLEEP WITH THE SPEED OF NOBITA FROM DORAEMON! IN ABOUT TWO SECONDS FLAT!
- LOVES TO TRAVEL THE WORLD. HE'S BEEN TO PRAGUE AND CHINA.
- PIERCES THOSE AROUND HIM WITH THE SHARPNESS OF HIS QUESTIONS.
- IN AN ARGUMENT, HIS WORDS ARE AS MERCILESS AND COLD AS ICE!
- ALWAYS THE FIRST ONE TO BUY THE LATEST TOYS...LIKE "THE CHALLENGER"! HE WORKS AS MY BETA--THE ARTIST WHO SPOTS THE SOLID BLACKS IN HAIR AND CLOTHING, LAYS DOWN THE HALF-TONES, COMPLETES THE BACKGROUND ART... AND IS A WHIZ AT SPEED LINES AND SPECIAL EFFECTS. HAS A WAY WITH PLANT LIFE...ON THE PAGE.

Number 49: Coward...!!

...ONE, TWO, THREE...
...ALL OF THEM AS DEAD AS STONE BUDDHAS...
THE RESULT OF SOME KIND OF NINJA SKILL...

BAD NEWS...

ULP!

STARTING OUT WITH A PROBLEM...
CRUD.
SNUFF
SCRATCH
SCRATCH

Number 49: Coward...!!

SIIIP

MMMM. NOTHING GOES BETTER WITH DANGO RICE DUMPLINGS...
...THAN OSHIRUKO BEAN SOUP.
AND AS SOON AS I'M DONE WITH LUNCH, I'LL GET TO THE TOWER...
...SO I CAN GREET ANYONE WHO MANAGES TO PASS THIS TEST.

FLIP
THE GOOD ONES SHOULD BE DONE...
...IN LESS THAN A DAY.

WHOP
AH... A COMPLETE KONOHA TREE-LEAF MARK!!

SHA
TERRIBLE NEWS, LADY ANKO!!
ZAAAM

!
ALREADY? WHAT IS IT?
DEAD BODIES! THREE OF THEM...

DEAD BODIES?!

DEAD... AND VERY WEIRD.
PLEASE, COME SEE FOR YOURSELF!

WEIRD... HOW?!
ULP!

JUDGING FROM THEIR BELONGINGS AND THE PAPERS WE FOUND, THEY WERE ALL SHINOBI FROM KUSAGAKURE--
--THE VILLAGE OF "THOSE WHO HIDE IN THE GRASS"-- AND WERE REGISTERED TO TAKE PART IN THE CHŪNIN JOURNEYMAN NINJA SELECTION EXAMS.

...
AND, AS YOU CAN SEE...

...THEIR FEATURES ARE COMPLETELY GONE...
...THE FACES AS SMOOTH AS THOUGH THEY'D BEEN MELTED AWAY.

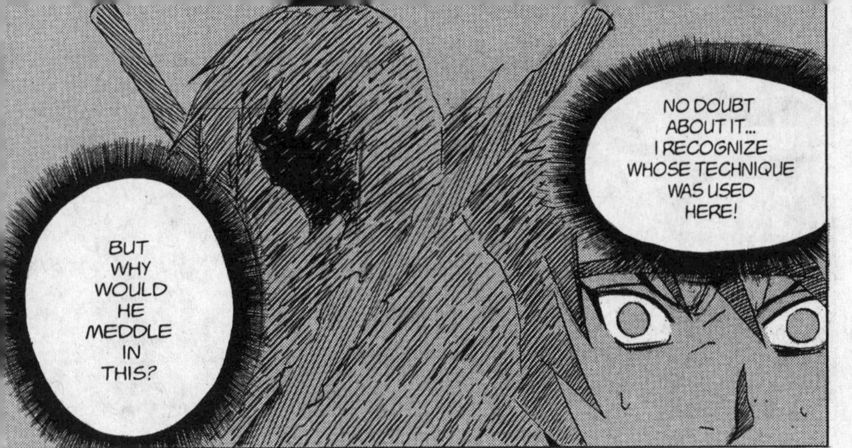
NO DOUBT ABOUT IT... I RECOGNIZE WHOSE TECHNIQUE WAS USED HERE!
BUT WHY WOULD HE MEDDLE IN THIS?

FWUP
SHOW ME THE PHOTOS FROM THE DEAD SHINOBIS' I.D.
AT ONCE!!

SO... THIS IS THE FACE HE STOLE...

BUT THAT MEANS HE'D ALREADY DONE SO WHEN...!!

THIS IS AWFUL!
WHAT?!
YOU THREE! REPORT WHAT'S HAPPENED TO LORD HOKAGE!!

ASK THAT HE DEPLOY TWO ADDITIONAL BLACK OPS TO THE FOREST OF DEATH AT ONCE!!
I'M GOING AFTER THE IMPOSTERS!

NARUTO...

ARE YOU OKAY...
...YOU BIG CHICK-EN?
!!!
R
RRR

AND YOU'RE THE IDIOT, IDIOT!
YOU'RE A COWARD. WHICH SASUKE ISN'T. SO YOU'RE NOT HIM!!!

!!
FWIIIP
!!
YAAAGH!

HEYYYY! GET OFF ME!!

HEH HEH... THE BRAT OF NINE TAILS IS STILL ALIVE AND KICKING!
FWUP

!!

FLIP
THERE'S THE PROOF. THE SPELL THAT SEALS THE MONSTER WITHIN APPEARS ON YOUR SKIN LIKE A TATTOO.

HOW FASCINATING THAT, WHEN HE IS CONSUMED WITH RAGE, HE LOSES HIMSELF... AND A BIT OF THE NINE-TAILED DEMON FOX TRAPPED WITHIN...
...COMES THROUGH. AN AMAZING DEVELOP-MENT!

POOM
POOM
POOM
POOM
木 TREE
火 FIRE
土 EARTH
金 METAL
水 WATER

SHK
A FIVE-PRONGED SPELL!!
SASUKE! NARUTO NEEDS YOU!!
UGK

LU.B
DU

BLINK

RUSTLE
OHHHH

AFTER BEING TRAPPED WITHIN HIM FOR A DOZEN YEARS...

...THE DEMON FOX AND NARUTO'S NATIVE CHAKRA AND PSYCHE HAVE APPARENTLY GONE FROM ENMITY AND OPPOSITION TO COEXISTENCE... AND ARE ON THE VERY BRINK OF SYMBIOSIS!

THIS SCROLL READS *TEN*, MEANING "HEAVEN."

BUT TODAY, YOU ARE MORE TROUBLE THAN YOU'RE WORTH.
天
SHF

FWIPP
HE'S BOUND TO FALL!!
NARUTO!!

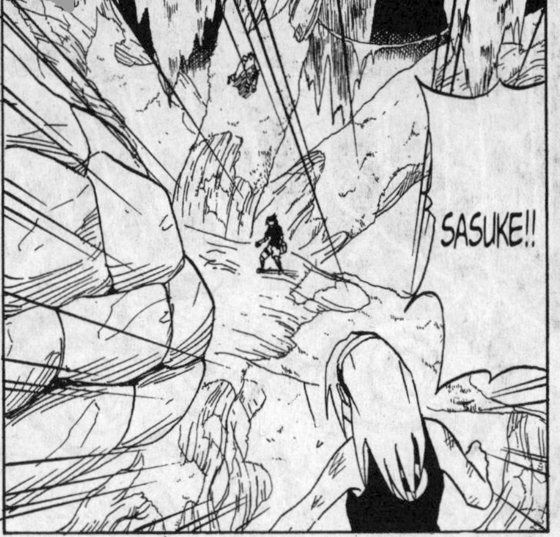
SASUKE!!

SNF

NARUTO MAY BE NOTHING LIKE YOU... HE'S CLUMSY, AND HE HOLDS US BACK...
AND SOMETIMES HE'S A BIG NUISANCE, BUT AT LEAST HE'S GOT GUTS!
NARUTO'S NO COWARD!
RIGHT?!

BABY BROTHER, YOU'RE PATHETIC. IF YOU WANT TO KILL ME, SETTLE FOR HATING ME UNTIL YOU CAN!
HATE ME... AND LIVE. LIKE THE COWARD YOU ARE!

CLING-ING TO LIFE...

...WITHOUT HONOR!

NO!!

HEH HEH... IT APPEARS THAT THE BLOOD OF HIS ANCESTORS IS RISING UP IN THIS ONE, DEMANDING ACTION.

SASUKE!!

WE'LL TAKE OUR TIME, SO YOU CAN SHOW ME ALL YOUR MOVES!
SWIPE

ONNNG

RUSTLE RUSTLE

GRAB
I'VE BEEN LIVING WITH THE HOPE OF ONE DAY KILLING MY OLDER BROTHER. I THOUGHT IT WAS THE MOST IMPORTANT THING...
BUT MAYBE I'M THE ONE WHO'S BEEN THE DUNCE ALL THIS TIME!
NARUTO... SAKURA...!
HOP
FWUP
FWUP
FWUP
...BECAUSE SOMEONE WHO CAN'T EVEN STAND UP AND DO WHAT HAS TO BE DONE AT A TIME LIKE THIS... WOULDN'T STAND A CHANCE IN A FIGHT AGAINST... *HIM!*
WHUP
THUNK
THUNK
THUNK
THUNK
KLAT

I SEE HIM!!
SMAT

FWAM
TOK
SHM
NOT BAD!
THE WAY HE ANTICIPATES MY EVERY MOVE... THE ACCURACY OF HIS TARGETING... HE SEES ME!
TWANG
FWUM
SKWEEEE
RRRRRRR
TWANG
VNG
STRING?
FWUNNG

A SHARINGAN "WINDMILL" -- A THREE-PRONGED ATTACK!
GOINNNG
SMAT
HE DID IT!!
...
!
HE FLAWLESSLY PERCEIVED MY ESCAPE ROUTE AND STRUCK ALONG A PATH I DIDN'T SEE MYSELF...
HEH... SUCH A SHAME...
FWUP
HAH!
HE MEANS TO USE THE ART OF FIRE-- DRAGON-FLAME TECHNIQUE!

SIZZLE
!!

FLASH

PUFF
HUFF
THAT ONE SO YOUNG SHOULD HAVE SUCH MASTERY OF THE SHARINGAN MIRROR EYE POWER...!
SIZZLE
TRULY, A WORTHY SUCCESSOR TO THE HONORED NAME OF CLAN UCHIHA!

IN FACT... I BELIEVE...
FLAKE
...I WANT YOU, AFTER ALL...!

SASUKE...!
TAK
HUFF
PUFF

SHRED
IT'S MARVELOUS FUN, HAVING YOU SHOW ME ALL YOUR TRICKS!

GASP
WE'RE PARALYZED!!
GASP

YOU REALLY ARE HIS BROTHER, AREN'T YOU?
YOU CAN SEE--AND CONCEAL--THINGS WITH THOSE EYES OF YOURS THAT ITACHI HIMSELF NEVER DREAMED OF!

!!

JUST WHO THE HECK ARE YOU?!

I'M OROCHIMARU, THE GIANT SNAKE.
IF YOU'D EVER LIKE A REMATCH...
...THEN PASS THIS EXAM AS QUICKLY AS YOU CAN!
SIZZLE

OH!!
THE SCROLL!

I'LL SEE YOU AGAIN, IF YOU MANAGE TO DEFEAT THE THREE OTONIN SOUND NINJA WHO ANSWER TO ME.
WH-WHAT ARE YOU BABBLING ON ABOUT?!
WE NEVER WANT TO SEE YOUR FACE AGAIN!

PERHAPS NOT... BUT WISHING WON'T CHASE ME AWAY.
FWUM

ZZUNG
!!
!!
CHOMP

...!!!

!!
SHLUK

Sh
...

SHHM
I LOOK FORWARD TO SEEING YOU AGAIN, SASUKE...
...IN THE QUEST FOR POWER!

OH!
WH-WHAT...? EVERYTHING... HURTS!
KNOT

CLENNnnnnn
CH
!!

JUST A LITTLE SOMETHING TO REMEMBER ME BY...
KRAK
SSHHH
POP

WHAT DID YOU DO TO SASUKE?!
SHFFF
POP
OWW!
KRAK
KRRR

?!

SASUKE!!!
!!
THROB
AAUGH!!

Number 50: I've Got to...!!
FIND THE LOVE...
...OF A LIFETIME!!

AAAAAAH!!
DUB

SQUEEZE

UNH...

AGH!!

AIIIEEE!!

SCRAPE

SOB

...

SOB

SHF SHF
SWUP
OHH...

AIEEE
EEE
PAFF
AIEEE
UNH...
OHH...

!!

UNNH...

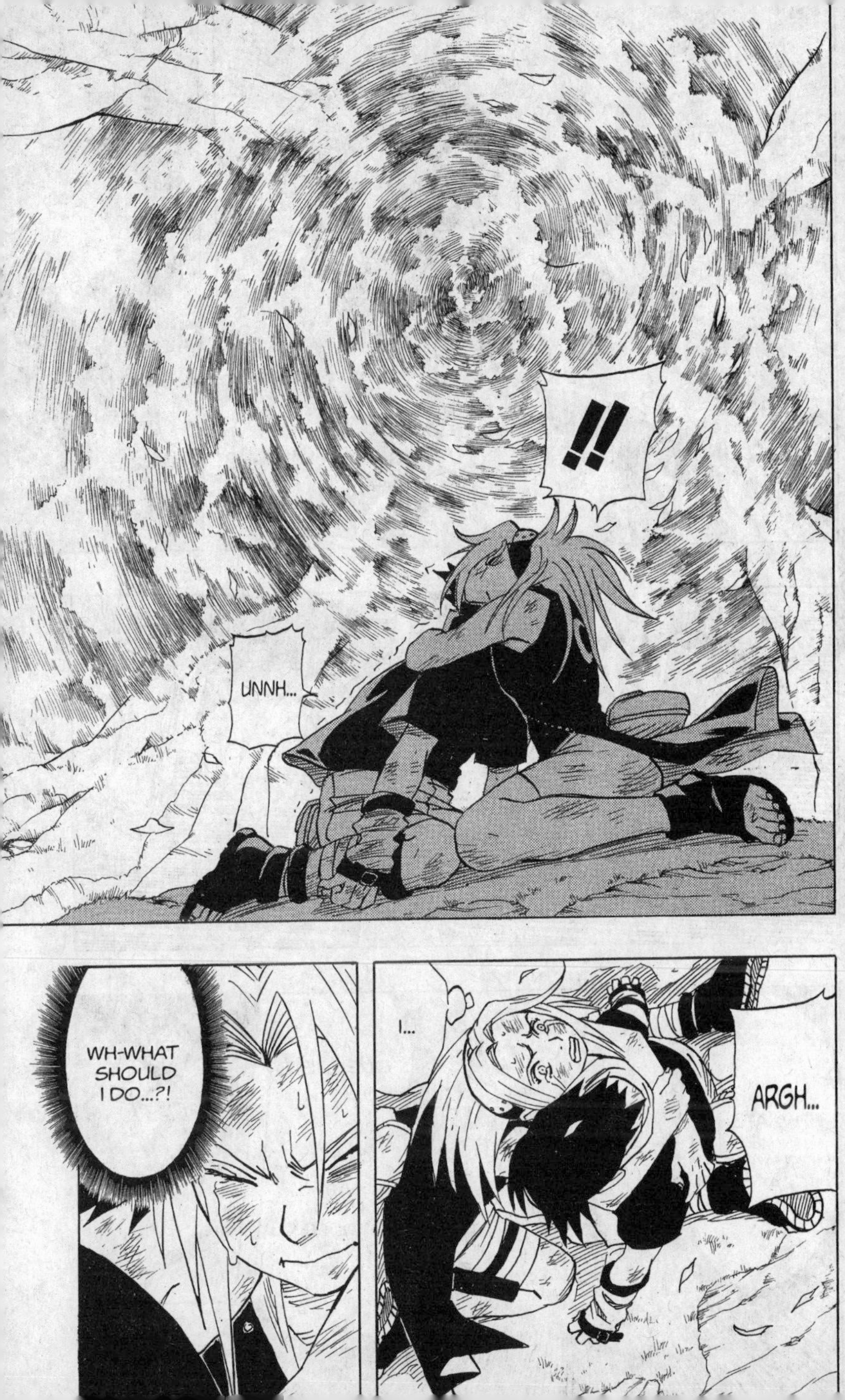

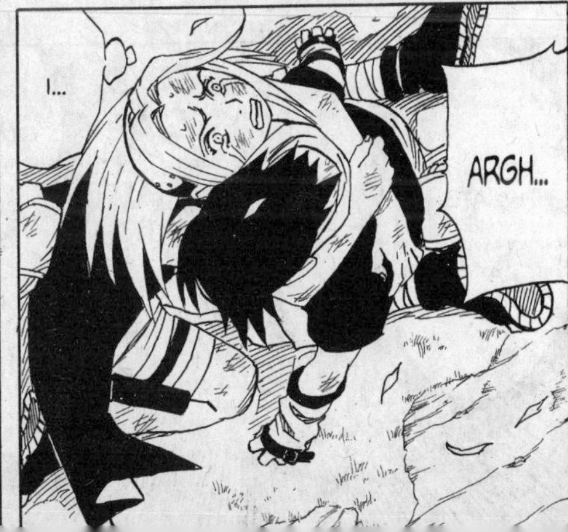
I...
ARGH...

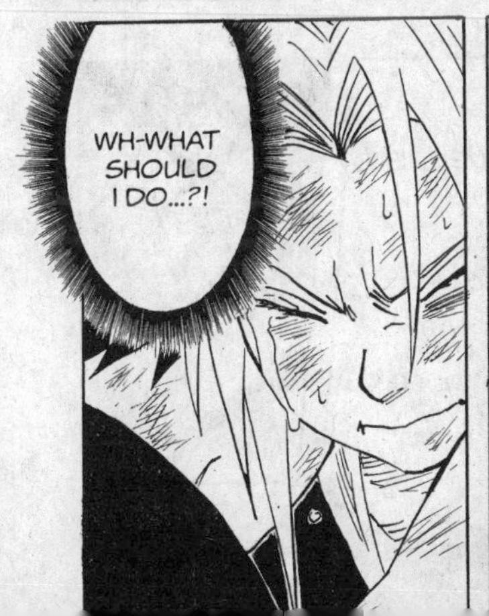
WH-WHAT SHOULD I DO...?!

TAK

IT'S ALREADY DUSK!

I HAVE TO FIND HIM SOON! THE DARKER IT GETS...
...THE WORSE THIS SITUATION WILL GET!
GRRRIT

THE QUESTION IS...
...WHY DID HE CHOOSE TO SHOW UP NOW?
WHAT'S HE PLAYING AT?!

TAK
TAK

NOT THAT IT MATTERS...
IF IT REALLY IS YOU, THEN WE'LL END THIS. RIGHT HERE. RIGHT NOW.

TAK
BECAUSE YOU'VE BECOME A BINGO BOOK, LEVEL S THREAT-- THE WORST KIND OF SECURITY RISK.
TAK

AND I'M GOING TO KILL YOU, EVEN IF IT COSTS ME MY LIFE!
AND IF I CAN'T MANAGE THAT, THEN...

TUMP
...AT LEAST I'LL SLOW YOU DOWN UNTIL THE BLACK OPS TEAMS CAN GET HERE.

SHHHF
IT'S MY DUTY. IT'S WHAT I LEARNED FROM MY GREATEST TEACHER EVER...

...WHAT I LEARNED FROM YOU...!

...ISN'T IT, OROCHIMARU?

IMPOSSIBLE...!

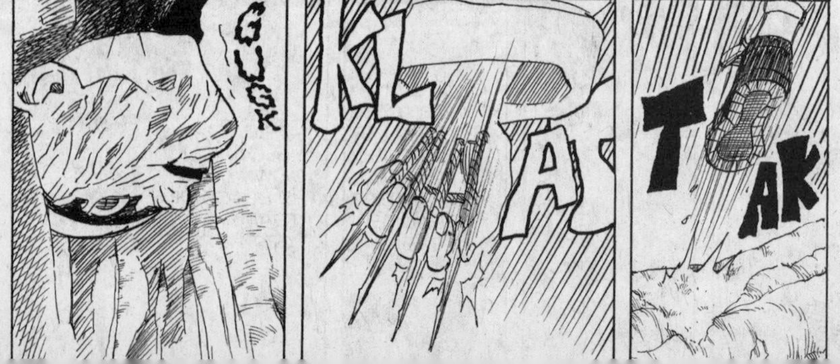

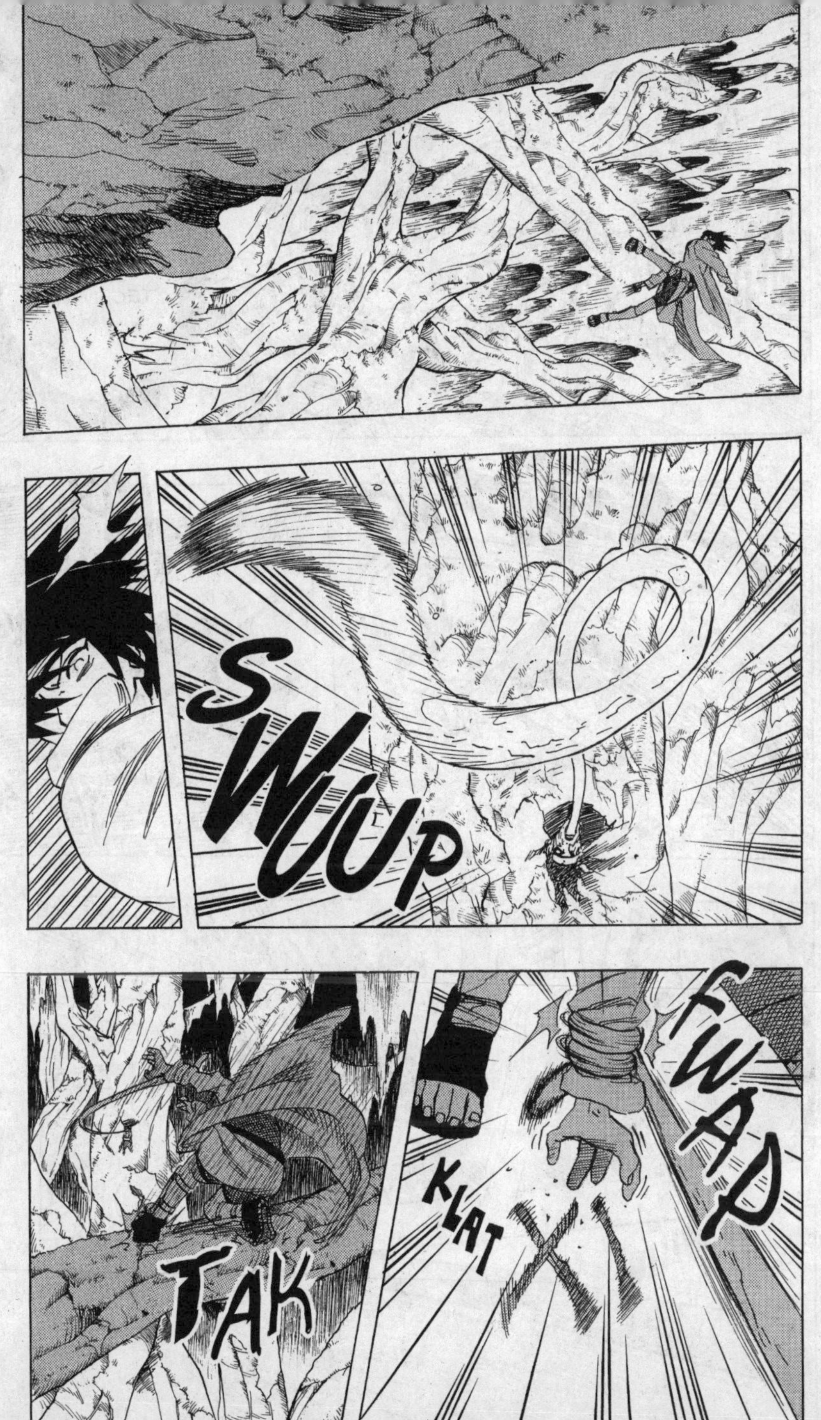

SWUUP
FWAP
KLAT
TAK

GOK
YOU CAN'T ESCAPE... STRIKING SNAKE TECHNIQUE!
KRNCH
HISSS
HSS

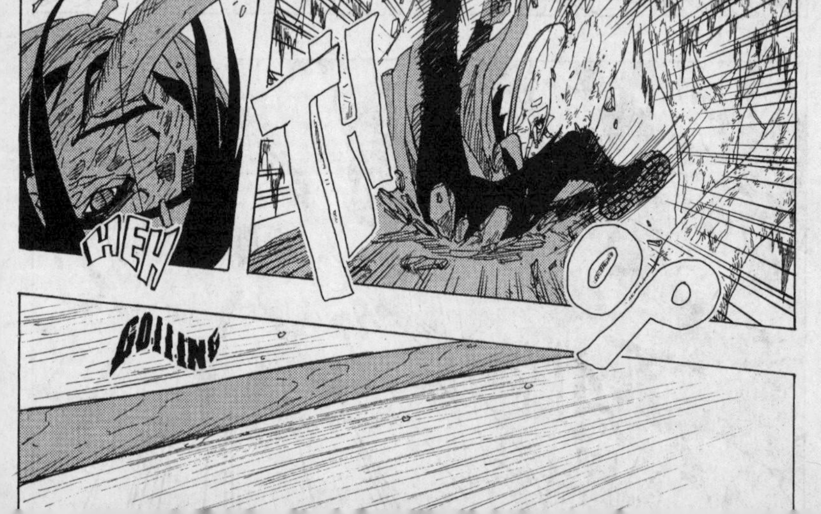

OHH!
KRAKLE
SHF SHF

SHLUK

HUF
HUF
HUF
HUF
!!
ONNG
GOT YOU!
OROCHIMARU, COULD YOU LEND ME A HAND? THE LEFT ONE?

THAT'S RIGHT... WE'RE GOING TO DIE TOGETHER. HERE.

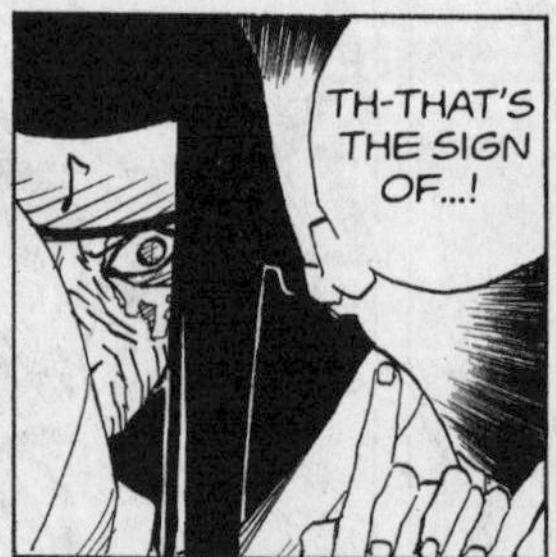

TH-THAT'S THE SIGN OF...!

ONNG

NINJA TECHNIQUE-- **"TWIN SNAKES KILL EACH OTHER"!**

YOU MEAN TO COMMIT SUICIDE? HOW PRECIOUS!

!!

BUT THAT'S A DOPPEL-GANGER...

!!

!!

POOF

SINCE, FOR THE TIME BEING, IT APPEARS YOU HAVE BECOME ONE OF THIS VILLAGE'S JÔNIN NINJA ELITE...

RRRIP

YOU MUSTN'T JUST...

SHF

...SQUANDER EVERY SECRET I TAUGHT YOU.

LUB DUB

WHY ARE YOU HERE? WHY **NOW**?!

WHY?

SNAP

FOR OLD TIMES' SAKE, OF COURSE, MY DEAREST ANKO! BUT FROM YOUR COLD REACTION...
...ONE MIGHT ALMOST SUSPECT YOU'RE NOT GLAD TO SEE ME!

OOOH...
WHAT IS IT? AN ASSAS-SINATION ATTEMPT? ARE YOU AFTER LORD HOKAGE?

HEAVENS, NO! I LACK THE HUBRIS-- AND THE PROPER NUMBER OF SUBORDINATES-- TO ATTEMPT ANYTHING OF THAT MAGNITUDE!
MY TARGETS ARE ANY NINJA OF THE VILLAGE WHO DISPLAY EXTRA-ORDINARY ABILITIES.

UHH...
UNH...
IN FACT, I JUST LEFT MY MARK AS A LITTLE PARTING GIFT...
SKRTCH
OHH!

...ON ONE OF THE BOYS.

UHH...!
YOU MONSTER!
HUF
IT'S A TIME BOMB... HE'LL BE DEAD IN NO TIME!
HUF
HUF

THERE'S A NINE OUT OF 10 CHANCE THAT YOU'RE RIGHT, OF COURSE...
BUT JUST THE SAME...
HE MAY SURVIVE... AS YOU DID.

AND THE THOUGHT OF HIM GIVES YOU...
...A CHARGE?
OH, MY DEAR! JEALOUS? AFTER ALL THIS TIME...
...ARE YOU STILL ANGRY THAT I USED YOU AND ABANDONED YOU?

UNGH...
THIS CHILD SEEMS QUITE EXCEPTIONAL... UNLIKE YOU.
HIS BLOODLINE IS THAT OF THE UCHIHA CLAN...

HIS FACE AND HIS BODY ARE VERY BEAUTIFUL.
HE COULD BE THE PERFECT VESSEL... TO SUCCEED ME.

UGH...
I FORESEE INTERESTING TIMES...
...ASSUMING HE SURVIVES.

AND DON'T GET ANY CLEVER IDEAS ABOUT TRYING TO END THIS EXAM.
...
SWIPE

I PLAN TO SAVOR THIS.
THREE OF MY PROTÉGÉS HAVE TAKEN THE PLACES OF THREE OF YOUR OWN.
SHHF

IF SOMETHING SHOULD HAPPEN TO ROB ME OF MY ENJOYMENT...
...IT WILL SPELL THE END OF KONOHA VILLAGE!
ONNG

HUF
HUF

IT'LL PROBABLY START TO GET LIGHT IN THE NEXT HOUR OR SO.
WE WERE ABLE TO USE OUR FIRST DAY TO SECURE FOOD AND WATER.
MNCH MNCH

MOST OF THE TEAMS WILL BE RESTING NOW...
...MAKING THIS THE BEST TIME TO ACT.

LET'S SPLIT UP...
...AND RECONNOITER FOR THE NEXT HALF HOUR.
BUT WHATEVER YOU FIND, WHEN THE TIME IS UP...

...BE SURE YOU'RE BACK HERE.
GOT IT?!

OKAY!

SNAP
ROGER!!

GOOD...!

LET'S GO!!

HOP

HOP

HOP

UNNH...

UH...

HIS BREATHING IS IMPROVING, BUT...
...HIS FEVER'S STILL SO HIGH!

I...

I'VE...
I'VE GOT TO PROTECT THEM BOTH!
GRRRR

HEH HEH... THERE THEY ARE!

AS LORD OROCHIMARU COMMANDED, WE'LL STRIKE AT DAWN!
AND OUR TARGET IS UCHIHA SASUKE!
IF THE OTHER TWO GET IN OUR WAY, WE CAN TAKE 'EM OUT, RIGHT?
OF COURSE!

MEET KISHIMOTO MASASHI'S ASSISTANTS--PART THREE
ASSISTANT NO. 3: IKEMOTO MIKIO

S.C.O.T. No. 3
ナルト
NARUTO
CONGRATULATIONS ON YOUR FIRST ANNIVERSARY! PLEASE KEEP WORKING HARD... BUT WITHOUT RUINING YOUR HEALTH IN THE PROCESS!
00.11.8
池本幹雄
(IKEMOTO MIKIO)

PROFILE

- LIKES SNACK STICKS AND COOKIES, AND EATS NATTÔ BEAN PASTE EVERY DAY.
- ADORES COFFEE. AT THE OFFICE, HE'S THE ONE WHO POURS.
- MASTER TINKERER.
- SHARP DRESSER.
- TALLEST ONE IN THE OFFICE.
- YOUNGEST ONE IN THE OFFICE.

} WE'RE SICK WITH ENVY!

WORKS AS A "MOB," DRAWING CROWDS AND BACKGROUND FIGURES, ADDING THE WHITE TO SPEED LINES, HIGHLIGHTS, AND CHARACTERS' EYES, AND WHITING OUT ANY ART THAT GOES OUT OF THE PANEL AND INTO THE GUTTER, AS WELL AS PUTTING STARS IN THE NIGHT SKY, AND ADDING IN HALF-TONES.

Number 51: Beauty Is the Beast!!

SPLASH
SPLASH

SQSH

PAT
GASP
GASP

ZZZ

RATTLE
RATTLE

I CAN'T LET MYSELF SLEEP...
...

OH!
IT'S ALREADY DAWN?!

TAP
!!
HUH?!

KLAT

LUB DUB

RATTLE
RATTLE

LUB DUB

LUB DUB

CRUNCH

!
A SQUIRREL ...?

WHAT ARE YOU UP TO, SCARING ME LIKE THAT?!
HOP

HEY!
CLENCH

HOP HOP
FWUUUP

!!
THUNK

THAT WAS CLOSE. THAT WAS TOO CLOSE!
SCRAMBLE
SCRAMBLE

SHE'S PRETTY TIGHTLY WOUND.
I WONDER IF SHE NOTICED THE LETTER BOMB WE STUCK ON THE SQUIRREL!
NO...
THAT'S NOT IT...

...?
WHAT THEN, DOSU? WHAT'S GOING ON?
...WE'LL HAVE TO GET CLOSER TO FIND OUT.

SO...
WHAT ARE WE WAITING FOR?
RUSTLE

HOP HOP HOP

TAP
TAP
TAP

FLUUUP
POK

TAP

...
FLITTER
FLITTER

...

OOMMMM
KRAKLE

IF I CAN CATCH...
...ALL 20 OF THESE LEAVES BEFORE ANY OF THEM HITS THE GROUND...

...THEN SAKURA WILL FALL IN LOVE WITH ME!!
BUT IF I MISS EVEN ONE...

...THEN MY LOVE FOR HER WILL NEVER BE REQUITED!
AND SHE'LL PROBABLY MAKE FUN OF MY HAIR!

LEE CREATES HIS OWN TRAINING EXERCISES, WHEREVER HE MAY BE.

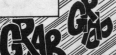

SHF
WHAM
BAM
YANK
ARGH!
!!
JUST ONE MORE TRY...
SHF
FLITTER
IT'S...!!
!!

READ THIS WAY

SKREE
SHRED
JUST IN THE NICK OF TIME!
A LETTER BOMB... ON A VERY SHORT TIMER.

WHO WOULD DO SOMETHING SO CRUEL?!

COME OUT OF HIDING... UNLESS YOU'RE A COWARD.
HOW'D HE SPOT US WHEN WE HID SO FAST?!
GRRR
GRRR
GRR

MY MASTERFUL PLAN A-- HIDING UNTIL ANYONE WHO MIGHT HURT US IS GONE-- HAS FAILED!
TIME FOR PLAN B!
STUPID PAIN IN THE NECK... FINDING US LIKE THAT!

RUSTLE RUSTLE
WOW... CAN I HAVE YOUR AUTOGRAPH?
OH! WHAT AN HONOR! LORD HYUGA NEJI, LAST YEAR'S ROOKIE OF THE YEAR... FANCY MEETING YOU HERE!
OH. IT'S YOU THREE...

GET A LOAD OF THIS!

FWISSSH
I CAN'T TELL YOU HOW LONG...
...I'VE DREAMT OF MEETING YOU!

IT MAKES ME SO MAD!!
WHY? WHY DIDN'T HE FIND ME SEXY? WHAT'S WRONG WITH HIM?!
I TRIED TO TELL YOU HE WOULDN'T GO FOR IT!

...
GET LOST.
SKF SKF

H-HOW COULD HE KNOW THAT... UNLESS HE DOES HAVE EYES IN THE BACK OF HIS HEAD?!
HEH HEH
O-OF COURSE NOT!

DOES THAT FIST YOU'RE SHAKING IN MY DIRECTION...
...MEAN YOU WANT TO FIGHT ME?
GLINT
HEY...

RUSTLE RUSTLE RUSTLE
O-OKAY!
HMPH... THEY'RE LIKE COCK-ROACHES.

I WOULDN'T DEMEAN MYSELF BY TAKING A SCROLL FROM LOSERS LIKE YOU.
IT WOULD MAKE ME A LAUGHING-STOCK.
THEN GET LOST!
GRRRR

HUF
PUF
HUF
PUF
HUF
PUF
HUF
PUF

LET'S GO SEE IF WE CAN PICK OFF SOME WEAKLINGS!
YANK
HOP
HA HA HA HA
I DOUBT WE'LL FIND ANYONE WEAKER THAN US!

SHIVER

HEH HEH... YOU'VE BEEN UP ALL NIGHT STANDING GUARD, EH?
GASP
!!
LUB DUB

SHHF
!!
TH- THEY'RE...!

AS OF NOW, YOU'RE OFF DUTY. JUST WAKE SASUKE FOR US.

THE THREE OF US WANT TO TAKE HIM ON.

LUB DUB
SHUDDER
SHUDDER
...?

WH-WHAT ARE YOU TALKING ABOUT?!
SHUDDER
SHUDDER

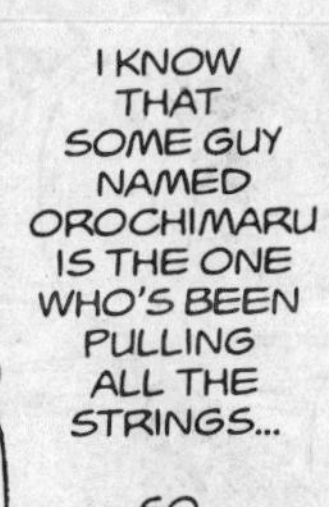

I KNOW THAT SOME GUY NAMED OROCHIMARU IS THE ONE WHO'S BEEN PULLING ALL THE STRINGS...
SO WHAT DO YOU WANT?!

?!
?!
?!

WHAT DOES THIS MARK ON SASUKE'S NECK MEAN?!

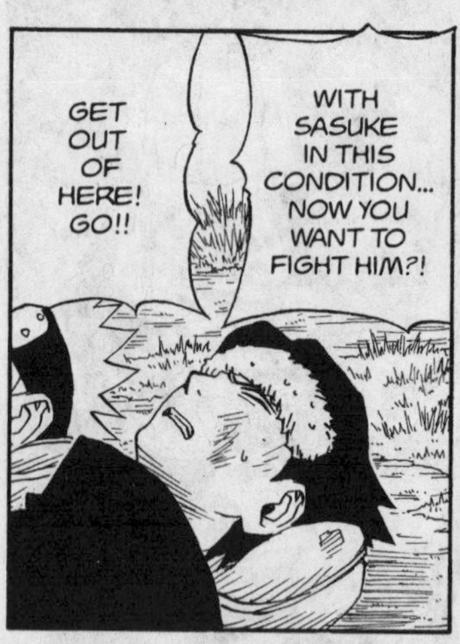
WITH SASUKE IN THIS CONDITION... NOW YOU WANT TO FIGHT HIM?!
GET OUT OF HERE! GO!!

...
HMM...
I WONDER WHAT OROCHIMARU'S UP TO?!

...?

WHATEVER... I CAN'T WALK AWAY AFTER HEARING THAT!
I'LL DESTROY YOU, GIRL... AND YOUR LITTLE SASUKE, TOO!

WAIT, ZAKU!
WAIT? WHY?

...

TAK TAK
FRESHLY TURNED STONES, EXPOSED SOIL...
GRASS IN A PLACE IT WOULD NEVER GROW...
SHF
IT'S OBVIOUS...

...

SOMEONE'S BEEN SETTING BOOBY TRAPS...
BUT WHAT'S THE POINT OF LAYING THEM IF YOU LEAVE EVIDENCE THAT WARNS YOUR PREY?
RRRIP

LUB DUB
GRR...

IT'S AMATEURISH!
SO... THE PERSON WHO THREW THE KUNAI KNIFE WAS TRYING TO STOP THE SQUIRREL FROM SPRINGING THE TRAP?
SHF
WELL, THE GIRL IS NO USE TO US...
...SO LET'S ELIMINATE HER FIRST.

FPP
FPP
TAK
!!
SHF
SHLUK

KRAK KRAK KRAK
VOOOOOM
A LOG?!
NOOOO!
THE TRAP WAS **ABOVE** US ALL ALONG!

POK
POK
POK
POK
TAP
VERY FUNNY!!
BLAM
!!
HUH?!
TO BE HONEST... YOU KNOW YOU'RE A COMPLETE NO-TALENT, DON'T YOU?
STOP DOGGING IT AND START WORKING AT IT!
IT'S AN INSULT BEING UNDER-ESTIMATED BY SLACKERS LIKE YOU!

POW
KONOHA HURRICANE TECHNIQUE!!!
WAM WAM WAM

?!
ACK!
SSHF
SHF
YIKES
TAP
?!
LOOK AT WHO'S TALKING...!
...
WHOA... IS THAT THE GUY WHO...?
TRY TAKING YOUR OWN ADVICE!!
WH-WHO ARE YOU...?!
KONOHA'S HANDSOME BLUE BEAST...
...ROCK LEE!

Number 52:

The Principles of Use!!

...!
WHERE DID YOU COME FROM?

I CAME...

...BECAUSE YOU NEEDED ME. AND I ALWAYS WILL!

!

ACTUALLY, IT'S THANKS TO MY LITTLE FRIEND HERE...
PAT
GO ON, NOW.

TAK
SSSSS

...

HUH?
...

I DON'T KNOW HOW TO THANK YOU. YOU'RE A LIFESAVER!
SHRUG
I PROMISED WHEN WE MET...

...TO PROTECT YOU... UNTIL DEATH DO US PART!

GLEAM
...!
I'LL PROTECT YOU WITH MY LIFE!

YES! I UNDER-STAND!
I GET IT, MASTER GUY!
...
KRUNCH

SHF

IT CAN'T BE HELPED...
ZAKU... LITTLE SASUKE IS ALL YOURS!
WHRRR
POK

THEY'RE AS GOOD AS DEAD!
TAK

FROM THE LOOKS OF IT...
...SAKURA DOESN'T HAVE ANY MORE FIGHT LEFT IN HER, EITHER.
BLINK
NHRRR
SHF

THIS UNIBROW KID IS OBVIOUSLY A VIRTUOSO OF THE TAIJUTSU PHYSICAL ARTS.
HE'LL MAKE AN EXCELLENT PLAYTHING.
FLAP

SHF
!!
THOK

THAM
?!!
POW

SHRED

!!

THIS IS SOME KIND OF ILLUSION, RIGHT?!
SO, I'D BE WASTING MY TIME DUCKING AS THOUGH YOUR ATTACKS WERE REAL.

!!
I'VE SEEN YOU USE THESE MOVES BEFORE.

HMF!
...
HE'S...
...SO STRONG!!

BUT THERE'S THREE OF THEM AND ONE OF ME, SO THEY HAVE THE ADVANTAGE.
IT'S A GAMBLE, BUT IF I TAKE THEM DOWN ONE AT A TIME...
MY STRENGTH SHOULD BE ENOUGH TO BEAT THEM!

RUSTLE
RUSTLE
GAAAAAH!
HOW CAN WE PICK OFF THE WEAK WHEN WE CAN'T FIND ANY WEAKLINGS?!

WELL ...
...BESIDES NARUTO'S TEAM, OF COURSE!
WHAT ARE YOU TALKING ABOUT, YOU IDIOT?!
!!
...
SNORT
WHAT?!
NARUTO AND SAKURA ARE TOTAL LOSERS...
...BUT THEY'RE TEAMED UP WITH SASUKE-- THE BEST OF THE BEST!

NOW, WHY IS THAT?
MAYBE YOUR PRECIOUS SASUKE IS BETTER IN THEORY THAN HE IS IN PRACTICE!

GRRRRR
ALL RIGHT, ALL RIGHT, SORRY FOR DISSING YOUR IDOL!

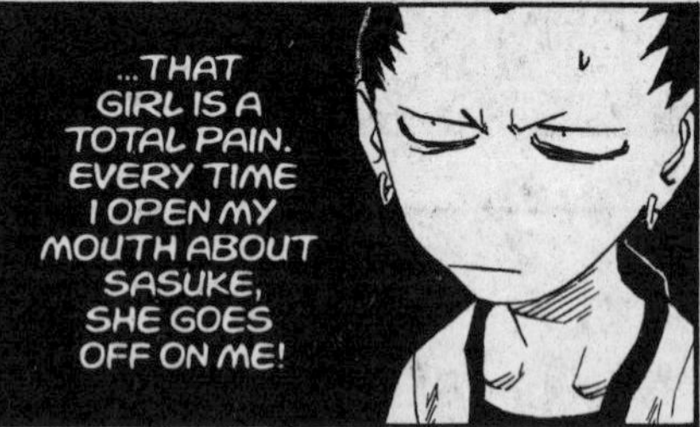
...THAT GIRL IS A TOTAL PAIN. EVERY TIME I OPEN MY MOUTH ABOUT SASUKE, SHE GOES OFF ON ME!

THERE'S NO WAY ANYONE HERE IS GOING TO BEAT SASUKE.
BUT SAKURA? SHE'S A COMPLETE WIMP!
HEY! SASUKE'S UNCONSCIOUS!

!!
AND SAKURA'S DEFENDING HIM.
GRRR

?!
OH!

IT'S NOT LIKE LEE TO KEEP US WAITING!
...
TAP
TAP

IT'S ODD... HE'S USUALLY SUCH A STICKLER ABOUT PUNCTUALITY.
...I WONDER IF HE RAN INTO TROUBLE...

NOT HIM!

NO WAY.

BUT WE SHOULD STILL GO LOOK FOR HIM.

RIGHT!
TAK TAK

I DID IT!
HUF
HUF
HUF
I FINALLY...
...GOT THE HANG OF IT!!
DON'T GO OVERBOARD!
WHOA
HUF
HUF
HUF
HUF
HUF
YIKES...
ULTI-MATE-LY...
...ONLY LEE WAS ABLE TO MASTER THIS TECHNIQUE, EH?

ALL RIGHT, LEE...
WOO-HOO!!!
I DID IT!!
I DID IT! ME!!
I REALLY, TRULY DID IT!!
STAGGER
HEY...

...
POW
YAAAH!
NOW THAT I'VE GOT YOUR ATTENTION, LEARN THIS WELL!
YES, SIR... WHAT IS IT?!
PLEASE SHARE YOUR WISDOM!
STAB
HUF
HUF

...
...
NOW THAT YOU'VE MASTERED THE *LOTUS TECHNIQUE*...
...IT WILL BE CLASSIFIED AS ONE OF THE FORBIDDEN ARTS!

?!
HUH?!

WH-WHAT ARE YOU SAYING?
!!

IT'S AN ART THAT DRAWS ITS POWER DIRECTLY FROM THE ENERGIES LOCKED WITHIN THE WIELDER'S CELLULAR STRUCTURE...
...SO WHEN YOU CALL UPON IT, YOU'RE SACRIFICING A PART OF YOURSELF!

NORMALLY, HUMAN BEINGS UTILIZE A MERE 20% OF THEIR OWN MUSCULAR ENERGY.
IF ANYONE WERE TO EMPLOY ANYTHING EVEN CLOSE TO 100% OF THE STRENGTH IN HIS MUSCLES...

...THE MUSCLES THEMSELVES WOULD QUICKLY BREAK DOWN ...SO THE BRAIN SETS A LIMIT ON HOW MUCH OF OUR OWN MUSCLE POWER WE ARE WILLING AND ABLE TO USE.

THE SECRET OF THIS TECHNIQUE IS IN OVERRIDING THAT INTERNAL CRANIAL SAFETY FEATURE, GIVING THE WIELDER ACCESS TO ALL OF HIS OWN CHAKRA.

DANGEROUS AS IT IS, THE RESULT IS THE RELEASE OF ENOUGH MUSCLE POWER TO ENABLE THE WIELDER TO PERFORM A SERIES OF GRUELING AND DEMANDING TASKS AT AN INCREDIBLE SPEED...

...PUSHING HIS OWN BODY TO THE LIMITS OF SAFETY ...AND BEYOND.

THUS, THE CIRCUMSTANCES UNDER WHICH YOU MAY EMPLOY THIS TECHNIQUE...
...ARE SEVERELY LIMITED.

SNAP
...
AND ...WHEN IS IT PER-MISSIBLE?
LISTEN CLOSELY, AND INSTRUCT YOUR MUSCLES...
...LIKE SO...

MASTER GUY... THE TIME HAS SURELY COME FOR ME TO USE THE FORBIDDEN SKILL YOU TAUGHT ME...
...AND NOT HOLD BACK!

HUF
!
HUF

TAK
HAH!

I'M DEFENDING THE LIFE OF SOMEONE WHO MEANS THE WORLD TO ME!

TAK

WHERE'D HE GO?!

!!

VZNN

!!

POW

SLLLIP
I'M NOT DONE WITH YOU YET!

VVN

FLAPPP
YANK

HE'S WIDE OPEN... CAN'T MAKE A MOVE TO DEFEND HIMSELF!!
OH, CRUD!
FWP
FWUP

AAAAG!!

TAKE THIS!
KRUNCH

FORWARD LOTUS TECHNIQUE!

HOP
BAM

!!
THIS... DOES NOT FEEL... GOOD...

...?!

WHEW...
LOOKS LIKE I MADE IT...

TAP

!!
NO WAY!
...WHAT A TERRIFYING TECHNIQUE...
I MANAGED TO LAND ON A PILLOW OF SOIL ...AND IT STILL ALMOST WIPED ME OUT!
RATTLE RATTLE

SHHF
SLUMP
OOF...

FWUP
BUT NOW... IT'S MY TURN...

!!
TAK

OH... THIS IS NOT GOOD...
HUF
THAT LAST MOVE I DID JUST TOASTED ME. I'VE GOT NOTHING!
HUF

SWOOP
HOP

SHUDDER
!!

!!

YOUR MOVES MAY BE FAST...

...BUT OURS ARE SUPER-SONIC!
AND MUSCLES ALONE CAN'T BREAK DOWN...
...THIS WALL OF SOUND!

SLUMP
UHHN...!

MEET KISHIMOTO MASASHI'S ASSISTANTS PART FOUR

ASSISTANT NO. 4: KAWAHARA TAKEMI

PROFILE

- A TOTAL PERVERT
- BLABBERMOUTH
- A NATIVE OF KANSAI WITH A GREAT SENSE OF HUMOR. (HIS OLDER BROTHER IS ALSO QUITE A JOKER. I'VE FALLEN FOR HIS PRANKS AT LEAST TWICE.)
- LOVES AMERICAN AND EUROPEAN-TYPE MUSIC.
- A TOYS"R"US KID AND A STAR CHILD.
- A REAL RAY OF SUNSHINE, HE BRIGHTENS UP THE MOOD IN THE OFFICE.

IN TERMS OF JOBS, HE'S AN ALL-AROUND MASTER OF ANYTHING AND EVERYTHING.

Number 53: Sakura's Decision!!

UWOHHH

!!

GAKK!
BLORTCH

LEE!!
KOFF
KOFF

!!
PLIT

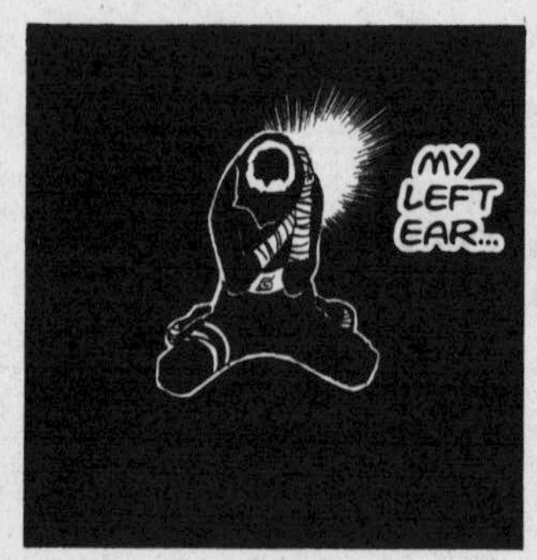
MY LEFT EAR...

IT'S THIS APPLIANCE ON MY ARM...
...YOU SEE? IT PREVENTS YOU...
KLAT
...FROM BLOCKING MY ATTACKS.

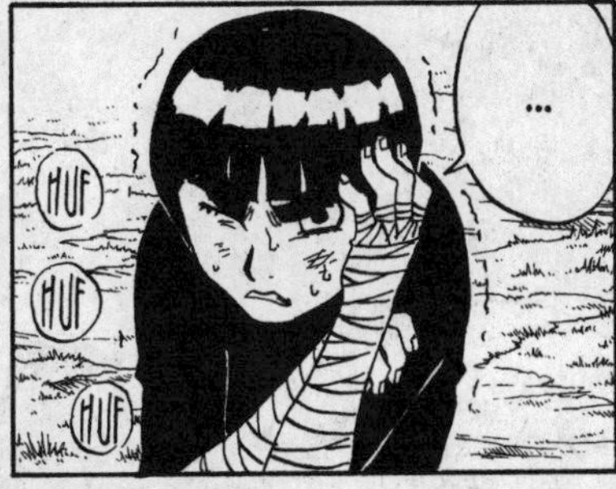
...
HUF
HUF
HUF

...!
WHAT DID YOU USE ON HIM?!

HEH HEH HEH...

IT'S SOUND!
EVEN IF YOU BLOCK MY FIST, THE SOUND WAVES REACH YOU.

SOUND?!

DO YOU UNDERSTAND...
...THE FUNDAMENTAL NATURE OF SOUND?

...!!

...!
VIBRA-TIONS ...?

PRECISELY.
YANK
WHEN YOU HEAR A SOUND, IT'S ACTUALLY...
...THOSE VIBRATIONS DISPLACING THE AIR, WHICH TREMBLES AGAINST YOUR EARDRUM.

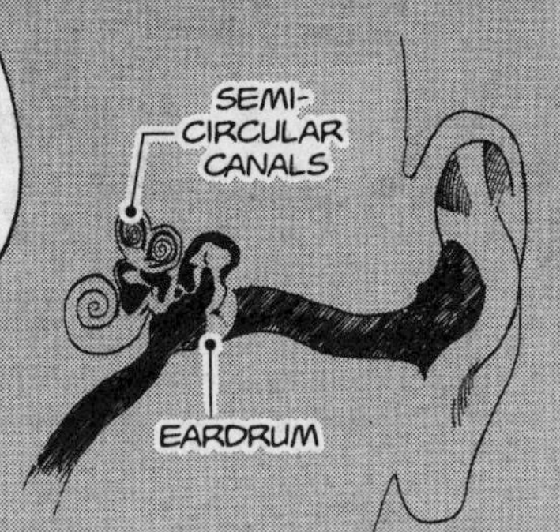
AND THE HUMAN EARDRUM-- THE TYMPANIC MEMBRANE--
...RUPTURES WHEN EXPOSED TO SOUND LEVELS IN EXCESS OF 150 PHONS.
MOREOVER, IF THE SOUND IS POWERFUL ENOUGH TO UPSET THE LIQUID WITHIN THE SEMI-CIRCULAR CANALS OF THE DEEPEST INNER EAR...
...IT BECOMES IMPOSSIBLE FOR YOU TO MAINTAIN YOUR BALANCE.
SEMI-CIRCULAR CANALS
EARDRUM

HEH HEH... AND IT WILL BE SOME TIME...
...BEFORE YOUR EQUILIBRIUM RETURNS.

SO, YOU SEE, CRUDE, OLD-FASHIONED PHYSICAL ARTS...
...SIMPLY DON'T WORK AGAINST US.

RRRRRR

YOU DID START OUT VERY WELL, THOUGH.
IT'S RARE FOR A FOE TO FORCE ME TO REVEAL THE NATURE OF MY TECHNIQUES.
BUT NOW THE TIDE HAS TURNED AGAINST YOU!
POP
POP

I CAN WIELD SOUND WAVES AS A WEAPON ...WITH ENOUGH FORCE TO CRUSH ENTIRE BOULDERS!
AND WITH A MERE THOUGHT I CAN USE SOUND WAVES TO FORCE AIR INTO THE EARTH BENEATH ME, TRANSFORMING ROCK-HARD SOIL INTO THE SOFTEST KIND OF CUSHION...
WAFT
WAFT
...A FAR MORE ELEGANT AND EFFECTIVE ART THAN YOUR CRUDE APPLICATION OF BRUTE FORCE.

OHHH

BLAST HIM...

THE ONLY TIME YOU MAY USE THIS TECHNIQUE...
...IS TO PROTECT SOMEONE VERY DEAR TO YOU.
...TO PROTECT... SOMEONE DEAR TO ME...?

!
PAT

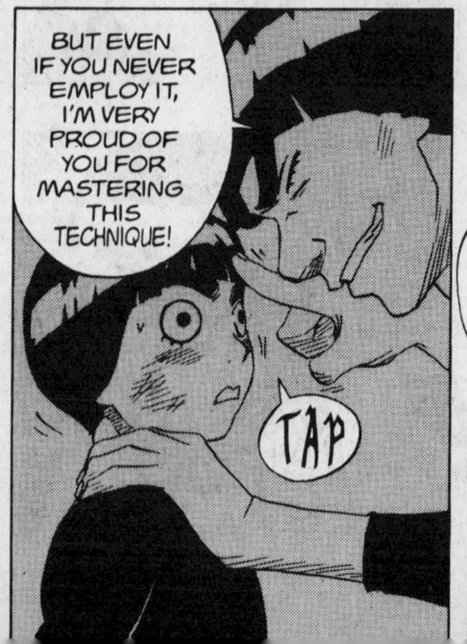
BUT EVEN IF YOU NEVER EMPLOY IT, I'M VERY PROUD OF YOU FOR MASTERING THIS TECHNIQUE!
TAP

GOOD WORK, LEE!
DARN IT...
FWUP
AND NOW...
...IT'S YOUR TURN.
TAK
!!
!!
BLAST...!!
HE'S COMING!
!!
!!
WHAT?!
FWUMM
FWUMM

IMPOSSIBLE!

LEE!!

KONOHA HURRICANE!!

EEP!

LUBDUB
UHN!!
MY LAST ATTACK IS FINALLY SHOWING SOME EFFECT!
!!
PAT

YOU STARTLED ME AT FIRST...

...BUT NOW, WHERE'S THAT FAST, LASER-SHARP ATTACK OF JUST A FEW MOMENTS AGO?

KRAK

OWW!

THOK

VIIN

HAH

VIIIN

THIS ARM OF MINE MAGNIFIES EVERY LITTLE SOUND FROM WITHIN TO THE UTMOST LIMITS. IT'S AN AMPLIFIER...

VIIIIIN

...AND IT GOES TO !!!!!
VIIIIINNNNNN
AND NOT ONLY THAT, BUT FAR FROM RELYING ON THE MOMENTUM OF MY ARM'S SWING...
...I CAN USE MY CHAKRA TO DIRECT ITS POWER TOWARD MY CHOSEN PREY, WHEREVER HE MAY LIE!!
LUBDUB
AAUUGH!!
LEEEEE!!

FWANNG

...OH ...MY...

SMAT

...

SMAT

SMAT

RUNNING AWAY SOUNDS LIKE A GOOD PLAN!
THOSE GUYS ARE GETTING CREAMED!!
IT LOOKS LIKE SASUKE AND NARUTO ARE JUST UNCONSCIOUS... BUT...

...THE FAMOUS LEE'S OBVIOUSLY HAD HIS BUTT KICKED, AND SAKURA'S ALL ALONE...
WHAT ARE YOU GOING TO DO, INO?!
WHY... WHY ARE YOU ASKING ME?

I MEAN, SAKURA'S IN DEEP! WE CAN'T JUST LEAVE HER.. CAN WE?!
WASN'T SHE, LIKE, YOUR BEST FRIEND OR SOMETHING?!

!
UM... INO?

WHAT'S UP, SAKURA?
I HEARD SOMEONE SAYING...

SAYING WHAT?!

SAYING THAT YOU LIKE SASUKE, TOO!

WHAT?

IF IT'S TRUE... THAT MAKES US...
...RIVALS!

WHY AM I REMEMBER-ING THAT NOW?
HEY! INO! WHAT'S IT GONNA BE?!

...!!
THERE'S NOTHING WE CAN DO. IF WE BLUNDER IN NOW...
...WE MAY JUST MAKE THINGS WORSE!

SHAKE SHAKE
THOSE GUYS WOULD TAKE ME OUT IN ABOUT 10 SECONDS FLAT!

NOT EVEN I...
...CAN BEAT THEM!

FWAP
!
FWUUM
SHF

HAH!!
SHINNG
SHINNG
VWOOOM
AIEE!!

MY THROWING STARS...
...WERE REPELLED BY A WALL OF AIR!!

HEH

!

KLAT
OW!!

OHHNG
!!

LOVELY HAIR... SO MUCH MORE BOUNCE AND SHINE THAN MINE HAS!
WHAT NINJA TECHNIQUE IS THAT-- THE ART OF DEEP CONDITIONING?

YANK
OW!
YOU'RE A DISGRACE TO ALL SHINOBI... FUSSING WITH YOUR LOOKS WHEN YOU SHOULD CONCENTRATE ON YOUR TRAINING!

ZAKU... WHY DON'T YOU FINISH OFF SASUKE OR ONE OF HER OTHER FALLEN HEART-THROBS...
...RIGHT IN FRONT OF THIS LOVESICK LITTLE PIG?
!!
THE LEAST WE CAN DO...
...IS ENTERTAIN HER!
HAH! GOOD ONE!!
YO!

NO! THEY WOULDN'T...!
HOLD STILL!
NGH!

S-SAKURA...
SKF
I CAN'T SUMMON ANY STRENGTH...
SKRITCH
SCRAPE

I...
PLIT PLIT

...I CAN'T...
I'M JUST A BURDEN TO THEM... JUST SOMEONE THEY HAVE TO PROTECT!

I'M ALWAYS IN THE WAY...
...NEVER HELPING. DARN IT!

I THOUGHT THIS TIME... IT WOULD BE DIFFERENT!
THIS TIME...
GRRRR

I NEED TO HELP THE PEOPLE I CARE ABOUT!

ALL RIGHT.
LET'S DO IT.

SHHHH

HEH HEH!
TOK

!!
HEY! SASUKE AND NARUTO ARE IN DEEP TROUBLE!

WH-WHAT'LL WE DO?!

RRRN
YOUR TRICKS ARE USELESS AGAINST ME, LITTLE GIRL.

YOU THINK SO?
HEH

CE
!!
WHAT...?!
!
!
!!!

Number 54: Sakura and Ino

I'D ALWAYS...
...THOUGHT OF MYSELF AS A FULL-FLEDGED NINJA...

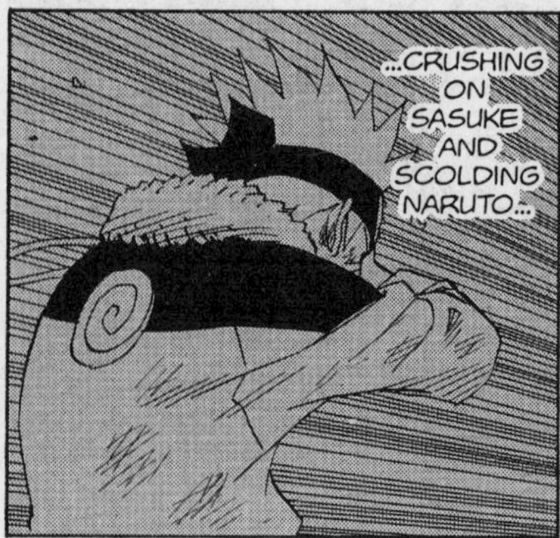

...CRUSHING ON SASUKE AND SCOLDING NARUTO...

...PROUD TO BE AN EQUAL AS I TRAILED AFTER MY TEAMMATES...

...WATCHING THEM...
...SAFELY, FROM THE BACKGROUND.

READ THIS WAY

WHILE THEY...

...WOULD BOTH RISK ANYTHING TO PROTECT ME.

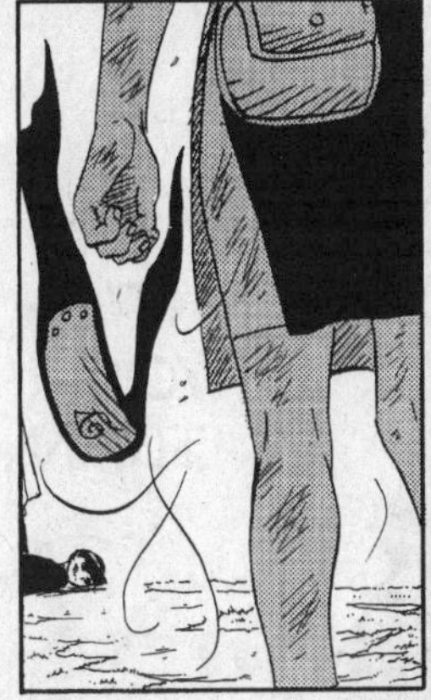

LEE SAYS HE LIKES ME, TOO...
UHN...

...AND HE RISKED HIS LIFE TO COME BETWEEN ME AND DANGER.

YOU'RE ALL MY TEACHERS...

...AND YOU'VE SHOWN ME WHAT I WANT TO BE...

...LIKE YOU. ALL OF YOU.
GRRR

NOW IT'S YOUR TURN...
...TO WATCH MY BACK!!
KIN! FINISH HER!!
!
...!
SAKURA...?!
HA!
!!

SWUP
SHHFFF

FWP
FWP

THOSE SIGNS SHE'S MAKING...!

TAK

ONNG

!!

...SHE'S MAKING A MOCKERY OF THIS, TRYING TO DECEIVE US WITH SUCH A RUDIMENTARY TECHNIQUE!
ZIGGING WHEN I ZAGGED...
SHA

THE ART OF SUBSTITUTION!!

THE NERVE OF HER, COMING RIGHT FOR ME!
KIN, LOOK OUT!
HOP
TAK
TAK

FWIING

GIVE IT UP.
THE AIR PRESSURE IS AT FULL STRENGTH, WITH NO ULTRASONIC OUTPUT...

SHFFT

POOR, FOOLISH GIRL... JUST A ONE-TRICK PONY.
PAHSH
PAHSH
ZANKUHA! THE BLAST THAT SLICES THE AIR!!
THOK
PAHSH
PAHSH
PAHSH
THUK

OBVIOUSLY...
FWUSH
...YOU'RE OVER-HEAD!

!!

FW UP

MY SMALLEST SKILL IS MORE THAN ENOUGH FOR YOU!!
FWIP
FWIP

TRY IT TWICE, TRY IT THRICE... THAT TRICK WILL NEVER WORK ON ME!
SMAT
KLAT

THUNK
!!
THU
THUNK

SHHF
HEH HEH...
SHHF
COME OUT, COME OUT, WHEREVER YOU...

...EH?
PLIT
!
PLIT

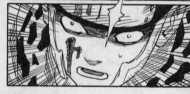

WHAT THE...?!

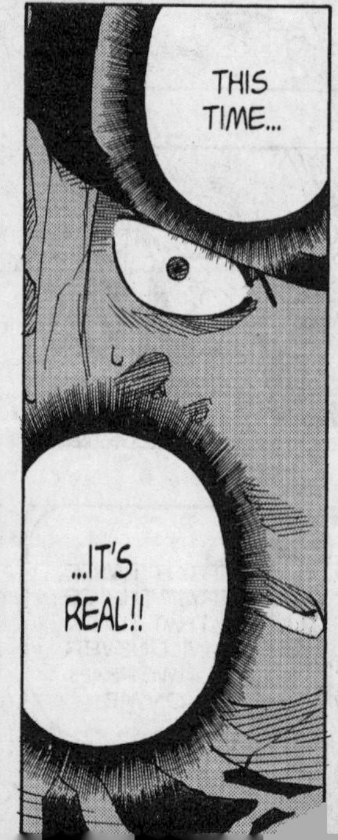
THIS TIME...
...IT'S REAL!!

POW

BOP BOP
BOP
KRUNCH
SAKURA...
SOB
SOB

EVERYONE ALWAYS CALLS YOU "BILLBOARD BROW," AND PICKS ON YOU...
!
HICCUP

...!
HICCUP
FLINCH
WHO ARE YOU...?

MY NAME IS YAMANAKA INO. WHAT'S YOURS?
I'M SAKURA... HARUNO SAKURA...

I CAN'T HELP NOTICING...
YOU DO HAVE A HIGH FOREHEAD...
...SO OF COURSE YOU GET TEASED.
TAP
FLUFF

AND YOU HIDE BEHIND ALL OF THAT HAIR... LIKE A SHEEPDOG...
...OR A SHY LITTLE GHOST.
FLUFF
SOB

!

TELL YOU WHAT, SAKURA... MEET ME HERE AGAIN TOMORROW, OKAY?
HUH?
I'LL MAKE IT WORTH YOUR WHILE... SO DON'T STAND ME UP.
TAK

DARN IT, LET GO!
SMAK
SMAK
GRRRRRRR

IT'S MUCH CUTER LIKE THIS, SAKURA.
YOU CAN KEEP THE RIBBON...

TH- THANKS... BUT...
BUT WHAT?
PEOPLE CAN SEE MY FOREHEAD!

THE ONLY REASON THEY TEASE YOU ABOUT IT IS BECAUSE YOU'VE MADE IT OBVIOUS YOU'RE SENSITIVE. DON'T PLAY THEIR GAME. SHOW IT OFF!

LET THE WORLD SEE THAT PRETTY FACE!! STRIKE A POSE!
INO...

HEY, INO! WHO'S YOUR NEW FRIEND?
THIS IS SAKURA.

SAY HELLO!
SHF
HOW DO YOU DO?

WHAP WHAP

HEY, EVERYONE... WANT TO KNOW A SECRET? THERE'S A BOY I THINK IS CUTE.
GUESS WHO IT IS!

WHAT ARE WE, MIND READERS?!
DON'T TELL ME IT'S SASUKE!

HOW...
...HOW DID YOU KNOW?

HEY...INO! SAKURA'S GOTTEN TO BE A REAL RAY OF SUNSHINE LATELY, HASN'T SHE?
...
WELL, DUUUH! SASUKE'S ONLY THE BIGGEST HEARTTHROB IN THE VILLAGE!
REALLY? SASUKE?

HIM! HAH!
HE JUST STRUTS AROUND, ACTING LIKE HE'S SO COOL.

HEY, INO! SASUKE SEEMS TO LIKE GIRLS WITH LONG HAIR, SO I'M GOING TO GROW MINE...

SAKURA...
EVERYONE SAYS YOU'RE AFTER SASUKE, TOO, INO...

I GUESS THAT MAKES US RIVALS...

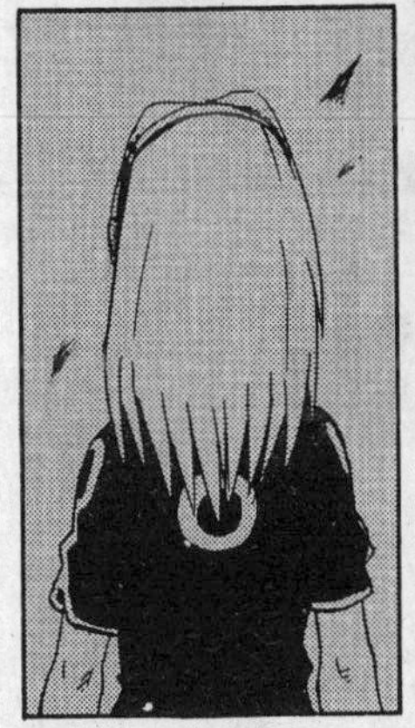

I NOTICE YOUR HAIR IS A LOT LONGER...
...INO.

WHAT'S IT TO YOU, SAKURA?!
FWIP
THINK YOU'RE SO GREAT? WELL, TOP THIS!
SASUKE AND I ARE ON THE SAME TEAM!
SIZZLE
SIZZLE
WHAT?!

SO, INO...
...YOU'LL NEVER BEAT ME NOW.

THAT GOES DOUBLE FOR ME, SAKURA...
...I DON'T CARE WHAT IT TAKES. YOU'RE NOT GOING TO SHOW ME UP!!

POW
POW

DRIP

UNHH

SMAK
THAM

TH-THIS IS NOT GOOD...!
INO! INO... COME ON!

THEY NEED ME... TO PROTECT THEM...
HUF
HUF
SKF
YOU LITTLE WITCH!!
FWUT

HUNH?

!!
!!

HMMPH! THE FREAK PARADE JUST GOES ON AND ON...

INO...
SAKURA... I TOLD YOU...
...I'D NEVER LET YOU SHOW ME UP!

IN THE NEXT VOLUME...

THE LAST CHANCE

Naruto's world begins to change forever as his teammate Sasuke is infected by the sinister mark of Orochimaru, the rogue ninja. But there's not time for dwelling on what may someday come to pass as the Chunin Exams kick into high gear. Does Naruto have what it takes to become a journeyman ninja? And if not, can he really ever expect to save his friends or protect his village? This could be his last chance to find out!

NARUTO 3-IN-1 EDITION VOLUME 3 AVAILABLE NOW!

STORY AND ART BY
MASASHI KISHIMOTO

In the years since the great ninja war, peace has bloomed in the ninja world, and a new generation has begun to take root. Naruto's work as an adult seems to be pretty mundane, but his son, Boruto, is constantly demanding attention. Luckily for Naruto, he can make clones of himself to babysit his son. But Sasuke's daughter, Sarada, could be the target of a mysterious figure who has connections to the Uchiha clan!

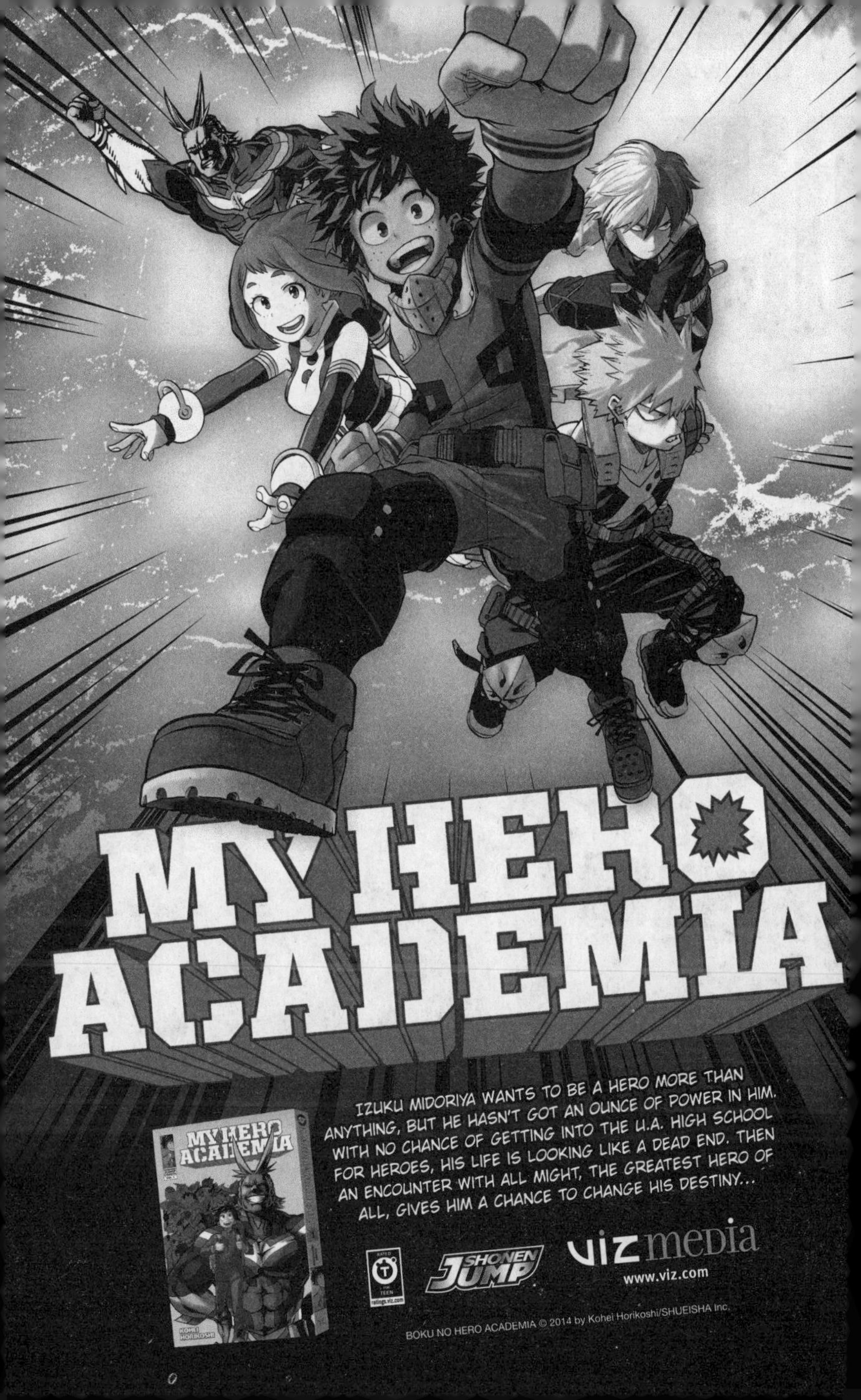